The Indo Immigrant

An Indo Man's Extraordinary Tales

Roy Van Westbroek

The Indo Immigrant

ISBN 978-1-105-03046-8

Book purchases can be made at: http://www.lulu.com/spotlight/roaddog60

For my family, present and future, may you always remember where you came from

Left to right is Connie, Mom. Louie, Ingrid, Roy, Dad, and Sylvia on the Zuiderkruis that took us to Holland in 1958

Rainbows Are Free

The sunset used to scare me when I was little, because I didn't know that the night was the same as day except for the absence of light, which sooner or later would appear as the moon brought forth its luminescence to cast its early shadows on things not yet seen or understood.

Rainbows are like that; they cast their brilliant colors on the shadows of life that have been drenched by the torrents of rain that only the weary traveler is aware of.

The heart returns to silence before its time, only to be reborn to pump its sweet melody through the veins of beings looking longingly for the essence that has brought it back once again.

Rainbows, like butterflies, are free souls remaining forever entangled within them. That's what makes a rainbow free.

Roy Van Westbroek

Table of Content

Acknowledgements

I have always wanted to write about my personal history and where my family had their roots. Although it seems that only famous people write their stories, I saw no reason that someone like myself would be less interesting to read about.

To my mom and dad, you have survived a long and difficult journey that only the hardiest of souls could have accomplished.

Finally to my brothers and sisters, and those immigrants that came along on our journey, it's been a hell of a trip.

1

The Beginning

Some people can remember the second that they are born, I; however, cannot. The only thing that I can remember was the howl of the stray dogs that ran behind our house on Ajoedija Weg in Bandung, Indonesia, as I lay awake in my room trying to sleep. That was when I was six months old.

My mom and dad had survived World War II, but unfortunately my grandfather Opa Rotschke did not, so I never had the pleasure of meeting him. Stories about World War II and the Japanese concentration camps would be one of my fondest memories of my dad. He would always take the time to sit me on his lap and tell those intriguing tales.

Indonesia at that time was a Dutch colony located near the equator between Singapore and Australia. It was a gorgeous tropical island. Being of Dutch ancestry, we had a privileged lifestyle. Apartheid was the law of the land, but I was unaware of this. As I was growing up, I began to notice that in this lifestyle I had a personal maid and someone to take me to school in my own horse and carriage. As with all such cultures, I had to go to a Dutch only school. Indonesia at that time was also going through a revolution to gain their independence from the Dutch. But I'm getting ahead of myself.

I have fond memories of my surroundings growing up in my earliest years. Our first house on Ajoedija Weg in Bandung was a nice single story dwelling typical of the style that was prevalent during the old colonial days. The place blended in well with the jungle. I can still remember that small cherry tree in front of our house that I would always try to climb but had no luck in doing so. As I remembered it, the rural areas of Bandung where we lived, was not as developed as the downtown sections better know as the "The Paris of Java", and other major cities like Jakarta. It had that rural feeling with its small dirt roads and surrounding jungle.

Sometimes during the week the food vendors would show up at the house and mom would treat me to the chicken porridge that the vendor would sell. It was magnificent with its thick broth, chicken, and vegetables. To this day I have never found anything like it, even though I have eaten in a lot of Indonesian and Chinese restaurants throughout my lifetime. One of the vendors would have lumpias, chitterlings filled with meat, and other weird foods that I couldn't get. I can still hear my Oma Rotschke haggling with the vendor over his prices. At that age I didn't know any better and depended on her and my mom to make sure I didn't get cheated, and I relied on them for everything else.

Besides my mom and oma, I had my sister Connie to contend with. Connie is a free spirited soul. Stubborn and wickedly independent, she would always give dad a run for his money. There were numerous times when she would set off on some type of excursion and be missing for several hours. This would drive dad crazy since he had to go and find her. Most of the time Connie would be at the kampongs, which were the Indonesian villages, a dangerous place to be considering the state of affairs that Indonesia was in. He would find her muddy and in disarray playing with the kids.

Connie can be mean at times. There was the time when dad was in the process of remodeling our house and somehow she found a handsaw, for some reason unknown to me she put a nice big gash on the side of my head with it. I must have provoked her. Screaming and bleeding I ran into the house. Dad, I'm sure, must have punished her, but I can't remember what happened.

There were also times when Connie would fight for me; for that I'm eternally grateful. In Holland there was a bully, typical Kaaskop, slang for a white Dutch person, who would hound me on a daily basis. One day as I was coming back from school he got a hold of me and painfully kicked me in the butt. Being out numbered there wasn't much I could do. So I told Connie and she proceeded to go down the alley to his house. Cursing and screaming, she challenged the young man to come out of his house to meet his maker. Of course being the punk that he was he laughed at her! Anyway he came out with his brother and friends to show that he wasn't afraid. Apparently he didn't know about Connie's fighting ability and reputation. She proceeds to beat the living daylights out of him. I had been redeemed. As I stood there with her older friends, most of them boys, the poor victim's father came out to see what the commotion was all about. I told him what had started this fight, and afterwards I was told he apparently had his turn with the young man. After that, he would never hound me again.

Connie has grown into a fine woman and has raised her family. She had her tough times and is now living in Oregon with her survivalist family and friends. She will always be my big sister that I love dearly.

Speaking of fathers, my dad Albert Van Westbroek was a hard working family man. He had survived the Japanese concentration camp during World War II. Out of the thousands of interns, he and his brother Ed along with a few hundred came out of the camp alive. The stories he would tell me were fascinating. Tales of hunger and Japanese brutality towards him and the others kept me intrigued, and I hung on to every word that he spoke as he told the tale.

One such story was about the day he was carrying heavy bags of sugar and stepped on a nail. His foot festered up, and when he went to the medical clinic he was told that they had to clean the wound out. This would be a very painful procedure; but if it wasn't done the foot would develop gangrene and would end up being amputated. There was no painkiller available, so they tied him down and gave him a piece of wood to bite down on and the job was done. I think dad was in his teenage years at the time, which is what probably saved him. He still has the scars on his foot.

During Indonesia's revolution, dad was an officer in the Dutch Air Force. My grandfathers were sailors in the Dutch Maritime Service, which might be the reason that our family ended up in Indonesia. As far as dad's father Opa Grillet goes, I have never met him, he left the family when dad was young.

Dad's mom, Oma (Moes) Grillet was a stern woman. She would always chase the girls out of the room when adults were in there talking, except of course me. I don't recall ever seeing dad in his uniform. Later on in my life, I found out that he was in the business of exporting and importing. This was when we were living in Bandung. Dad was planning to leave Indonesia for Holland to escape the aftermath of the Indonesian revolution.

What can I say about mothers? I have been told that when a man dies in battle he would more than likely call out his mother's name. My mom Amelia was my whole world in those early days of life. I depended on her for everything.

Amelia was also a survivor of World War II, but she didn't go into the Japanese concentration camps. Her mom, Oma Rotschke, her sister Jane, and brother (Boy) Ernest were able to flee the Japanese, and took a new name in order to escape internment. Unlike dad she was lucky. Oma Rotschke was my favorite grandmother. Opa Rotschke died in 1945 during World War II from complications he experienced under the Japanese occupation of Indonesia.

Married at an early age, my mom Amelia would end up with three daughters, five sons, and a large number of grandkids and great grandkids. Being used to the privileged lifestyle in Indonesia, the relocation to Holland and then the United States was difficult for her. The transition from hot tropical island weather to the cold gray wintry one in Holland was unbearable. It was for me.

After we left Holland, America became our home. It would take mom years to learn the English language, but she did. She remains the rock of stability that our family and I have always depended on.

This is what I remembered of my earliest years growing up in Indonesia before our immigration to Holland, and America; a time before I had my sibling sisters and brothers. It was also a time that seemed uneventful, but would ultimately shape my life's values.

The landscape surrounding Bandung, Indonesia, during my earlier years, was magnificent.

Pictured are Roy and Mom when we were living on Ajoedija Weg in Bandung, Indonesia, in the 1950s. In the background is the cherry tree.

2

Living in Bandung

The move to the big house on Pasteur Weg in Bandung, Indonesia, didn't stand out in my memories, all I remembered was that one-day I woke up in a new house that was bigger, and had a huge front yard with the jungle bordering our back yard. It would be a time when my Oom Boy, mom's brother, would take me to the kampongs, and of riding my first motorcycle. Unfortunately I would also be exposed to the tragic aftermath of war. It was a time of growing up and becoming aware of what was right and wrong in this world of mine.

Our big new house looked like one of those plantation type mansions with the giant entryway doors. The foyer was huge and led into a large living room. This room would hold some strange memories for me. Here is where my mom and dad would place the great big Christmas tree with its little white candles and the ornaments. This is also where I would meet Sinter Klaas and Swarte Piet two of my most dreaded persons in my young life. A lot of pleasant and unpleasant memories would be made in this great old house.

In the front yard there were palm trees and various types of fruit and shrubbery. Along the front of the yard was a little retaining wall made from small bricks about three feet high and on the other side by the street ran a little creek. I would play with my homemade toy boat and float it down the little river that was created during the monsoon season. This is also the same place where I viewed some disturbing scenes.

On the side yard is where we kept the chicken coop and pigpen. We had a mean dog and dad kept him leashed in the side yard. I was terrified of the brute and on more than one occasion I would torment him on the urgings of Connie to prove how tough I was. For this he bit me more than once. I have always remained wary of the German shepherd.

Beyond the back yard gate the jungle began. It was a place that held a great mystery for me, and I was forbidden to enter it alone. My Oom Boy would always dare me to go in there, but I knew dad would raise hell with me if he found out. During the night I could hear the monkeys wail away and the sound of the jungle birds cuckooing. There would also be the fireflies that we caught and put in a mason jar to show off to our friends. Some friends say that they heard the tiger too, but I don't give it much credence.

I had a good life in this house. Mom and the maids were excellent cooks. Indonesian food has a taste all its own. Sometimes dad and I would harvest the honey from the hive that was attached to the overhang of the roof. Dressed in his beekeeper outfit, I would watch him smoke the bees into a state of calmness and gather up the delicious nectar

The only thing I didn't really like was butchering the chickens. My first attempt at this was a disaster. Oom Boy would catch the chicken, and egged me on to go ahead and prepare the bird. I was reluctant, but his heckling of me drove me mad and I proceeded to stretch the chicken's neck on the cutting stone. Using the cleaver, I swiftly chopped off its head. All of a sudden the headless chicken ran around the yard blood spurting from its severed neck. I was mortified, but my oom was delighted of my manly task. At the age of five, I wanted to please my oom. After this, I would let the cook do the butchering.

During the Fifties we had no television or computers. We made our own toys. With my oom's help I made a sling shot from a tree branch shaped like a **y**, a couple of strips of old inner tube from a bicycle tire, and a piece of leather from an old shoe tongue. The great hunter had arrived and in my shorts and tee shirt, barefooted, I would go on the hunt for dangerous game. The hapless birds would mock me with their chatter as I continued to miss them. Nevertheless, I enjoyed my adventures of the big hunter in our tropical paradise.

The kampongs in our area were mysterious places and one day my Oom Boy sneaked me into the village. Little did I know that he had an ulterior motive. Oom Boy was a tough Indo man who relished in the Spartan way of life. He would always dare me to do things. Being mom's younger brother he would always take me under his wing, since I was the only boy in the house.

For some reason he started to train me in boxing, which made my Oma Rotschke and mom furious, but that didn't stop him. Due to dad's war experience, dad tried to keep me away from violence. Dad was a busy man with his exporting and importing business, so I was sure he didn't know what was going on. Feeling that I was ready, Oom Boy took me to the kampong. When we arrived they had set up a boxing ring in the middle of the small dirt square. Animals were running around loose, and the smell of food cooking permeated the air. Now I knew the reason he had brought me. My turn came, and I boxed fearlessly; missing most of the blows I threw at my equally hapless opponent. After a few minutes, with face-flushed red from exhaustion and my arms limp, the match was called a draw. Oom Boy didn't make a dime. Oma Rotschke was furious, but the lumpias she gave me made up for it all.

Christmas was a time of magic. On the night of the event my sisters and I would stand in the front yard looking for Santa

Claus and his helper riding their sleigh in the night sky. In those days I never saw or met a black man, and our Swarte Piet, Santa's helper, was a white person with black face makeup. I never did spot them.

On Christmas Eve the family would gather around the Christmas tree. It was huge, reaching all the way to the top of the ceiling, and was decorated with little white candles and elaborate homemade decorations. As I sat there, I was in mortal fear of being put into Santa's toy bag by Swarte Piet. It was common knowledge with the children that bad kids would be put into Santa's bag; they were never seen again. This was Swarte Piet's job, and he knew who the culprits were.

The moment of dread had come; it was my turn to answer for my misdeeds. Shaking and with wobbly knees I moved forward towards Sinter Klaas. I was shocked; in his hands he held a great big list of my misdeeds, with a loud boisterous voice he ordered me into the bag. The bag was dark, and I screamed for mercy. After what seemed like hours, I was finally released from my terrible prison. Everyone laughed. In my later years, I realized how precious those moments were, but back then I was mortified.

I've always loved the stories that dad and my oom would tell me. Besides the stories about the Japanese camps there was one about the time that Tante Lily, mom's sister, and Oom Ed, dad's brother were kidnapped by the Indonesian extremists who came from the southern end of Bandung. Apparently, according to mom, the city was divided into north and south sectors with the railroad tracks being the dividing point. Above the tracks by the mountains was the northern section, controlled by the Dutch, and the southern section had the Indonesian extremists, and also the British.

Once it was found out that they were missing, dad and Oom Jack went to find them. Disguised as Chinese men they went down south and did an extensive search, and found both of them alive. Luckily for Tante Lily and Oom Ed the British had arranged a prisoner exchange with the Indonesian extremists. I can only imagine the sheer joy that the family felt.

Indonesia's revolution had a profound impact on me in those younger years. One day, as I was playing in the front yard, I saw this monstrous tank roll by on the street in front of our house. Mesmerized by the deafening roar of the engines and tracks, I ran up for a closer look. The tank had mud all over it and the tracks had clumps of red clay stuck to it.

Years later, when I was older, I realized that the clumps were parts of the human body. Mom also told me at that time, that she had stopped letting the maids do the cooking for fear that they would put ground up glass, or bamboo splinters into the food.

Those early experiences would be my first look at war in my lifetime.

Other than those fearful and sad moments, there were happier ones. Once a month dad would take me to get a hair cut. The barber had his shop in a building with a thatched roof made from palm fronds, which was located in a small village next to a stream. After the haircut, I would always be treated to a bowl of boiled noodles with chicken or meat, and vegetables. One of those fine days I decided to add some sambal, Indonesian hot sauce, into the noodle dish, well I overdid it and started choking on the soup, tears running down my cheeks, and my face turning red. Of course I pretended that I could finish the bowl, but after a while dad told the cook to get me a fresh bowl.

Besides getting haircuts and hot bowls of noodles I remember going to the Tangoengprau Volcano in Bandung, dad and Oom Boy would buy canaries in little wooden cages before we set off around the rim of the volcano. Down we would go into a steam filled cauldron with the smell of rotten eggs all around us. They told me the reason for the canaries was to let us know when it became too dangerous to go down any further. The canaries would apparently die before we did. I never saw any of the canaries die.

I went on with my life in Bandung with little or no worries. School was pleasant, and I became proficient in Dutch and the Indonesian language. I would be taken to and from school in my own personal bejack, a sort of horse drawn carriage. I didn't realize at the time that apartheid existed and that being Dutch had its privileges.

This was about to change, and in December there were signs around the house that dad was relocating us to Holland. I don't recall the exact dates, but sometime in early January 1958, we went to Jakarta to be packed on buses to take us to our ship the Zuiderkruis, an old World War II medical ship. It seemed that my privileged life was coming to an end. Everything the family had was taken away. So with not much more than our clothes and some personal belongings we boarded the ship and sailed for three weeks to Holland.

Life onboard the Zuiderkruis was exciting. The smell of the ocean, flying fish alongside the boat, and watching the gorgeous sunrise and sunset on the endless horizon, instilled in me a longing desire to become a sailor.

Dad and the other men were given tours of the engine rooms and the ships galley. They also attended dances and other functions to keep them from going stir crazy onboard ship.

After we sailed through the Suez Canal and the Mediterranean Sea past the Rock of Gibraltar, we ended up on the Atlantic Ocean and then the North Sea. A storm was raging, and everyone on board got sick from the wet weather, we had arrived in Holland. I was getting older, and I would have some fond memories of living in Holland.

Left to right; Connie, Mom, and Roy in the early Fifties, Bandung, Indonesia

Mom and I in Bandung on Ajoedija Weg

L-R Tante Jane, Oom Ed, Connie, Mom, Oma Rotschke, Oom Ben and friend in front of the house on Pasteur Weg

Roy and Connie with the Koender's maid in the front yard of their house in Jakarta, Indonesia

Oom Koenders, Tante Lucy, and Luke at their place in Jakarta

The family is photographed in front of the house on Pasteur Weg in Bandung, Indonesia. Mom's motorbike is shown in foreground.

Wedding picture is taken by the large entryway to the big house on Pasteur Weg in Bandung, Indonesia. Roy and Connie are sitting in front. Oom Boy is standing on the far left.

3
Life in Breda, Holland

On a gray wintry day the Zuiderkruis moored at the docks, I can't remember if it was in the Port of Amsterdam or Rotterdam. The last few days were tiring, and I was not feeling too well. I had missed breakfast a couple of times because I woke up too late. The food onboard ship had been good, especially the snacks. Dad had given me a Coca Cola for the first time in my life. The taste was unusual, and I wasn't used to the carbonated drink. I could honestly say I didn't like it. Somehow I managed to get up in time that day to get something to eat before we docked.

There isn't much I can say about the trip from the docks to our house in Breda, Holland, simply because I can't remember anything about it. Our house was located on 46 Heemskerk Straat. It was a cookie cutter three-story house made of brick, and looked like the rest of the houses on the block. Across the street from our house was a Catholic school; down the street, located in the middle of the block as you walk east, there was a worn out grass field; further down the block as you go west there was a soccer stadium; about a quarter mile south from our house was a canal. The weather was cold and gray.

Holland is located off the Atlantic coast where it is cold most of the time. Compared to Indonesia it was a dismal depressing place. The landscape consisted of farmland, no mountains, and most of all none of the tropical jungle foliage and rivers. I couldn't imagine having to live here for the rest of my life. The Hollanders themselves were different. They were fully dressed and had on shoes, apparently to ward off the cold weather. When I lived in Indonesia, I wore shorts and sometimes a shirt, but hardly ever did I wear shoes. I was turning eight years old this year, and I could sense a feeling of dread as I began my journey of assimilating into the Dutch culture. It would be a time of great discovery and personal growth.

Life in Holland, specifically Breda had its memorable moments, and challenges. Of course the biggest challenge of all was going to school. I wasn't used to being all dressed up in my long woolen pants and shirt. The knee high black boots were uncomfortable, and the beret on my head made me look like a Frenchman. So off I went with Connie to our new school.

The school was about half a mile from the house. To get there we had to walk through some fields and past a small pond. It was cold and drizzling that first day. I don't recall what grade I was in. Most of the kids in my classroom were Dutch with some Indo's and a few other races mixed in. So I began my studies of reading, writing, and arithmetic. At eight years old I really didn't care that the ruling class of Holland was called the House of Orange. The history lessons that I had any interest in were the histories of Holland during World War II: the Dutch underground during the Nazi occupation, and the Dutch naval heroes. They were all stories of adventure.

One of my favorite things in school was what happens during a person's birthday. On that day the lucky kid could bring candy to school and after sharing it with their classmates, he or she gets to visit other classrooms and share the candy with friends. Here was the chance to get even with the school bullies or the snobs that hounded you on a daily basis. They would have to watch as everyone else got their candy. It was justice for the little person. Needless to say everyone became your friend that day.

Sports in school consisted of playing soccer, basketball, and running around the playground. Most of my soccer playing was done on the small field by our house with the Indo friends I had. We would always challenge the Dutch boys in a game that usually ended up in a fight. This was also the place that for the first time in my life I would hear racial slurs concerning my ethnicity. Up to that point I didn't notice that I was any different than the rest of the kids.

Playing basketball at school was something else. Compared to today's standards our basketball equipment was archaic. Instead of the high tech backboards and scoring system, we had an actual wicker basket mounted on a pole. The basketball was made from cowhide. Under the watchful eye of our teacher we played the game. There were no fights during these games; school was where civilized persons went.

Breda was a small dorp when I lived there with my family. It was a place for working families. There was only one family on the block that was financially well off enough to have a car and most of all a refrigerator that we could get ice cubes from. They were of course the most popular kids on the block, if not the neighborhood.

In the town square was where the butcher, grocer, cafe, and I think the ice cream parlor did their business. I had figured out a way to get free scraps of meat; mostly end cuts of bologna, salami, and whatever else the butcher had if I told him it was for my dog. Usually there was about a quarter pound of the stuff given to me. I'm not sure if my parents ever found out about it. My favorite treat was when dad would take me to get pat tat frit, also known as French fries, at the ice cream place. The owner would put it in a small cone shaped paper bag and pour mayonnaise all over it. Other than these occasions we hardly ever ate out on the town. It was a working family town, and dad worked hard to give us a life that closely resembled what we had lost.

Whatever free time dad had he would spend with mom and the kids. I remember fondly the trips that I would occasionally take with him. My most memorable trip was the one to the Ryks Museum in Amsterdam. Here was where I would intensely stare at 17th century Dutch art collections, my favorite being "The Night Watch" by Rembrandt. There were many such delights throughout the building. Afterwards we would go to one of the Catholic cathedrals and go inside. Once inside, I would marvel at the interior decorations of elaborate religious paintings depicting Christ's birth, his crucifixion and resurrection, and the apostles. Naturally there were also statues made of gold, and uncomfortable benches made of oak.

Sometimes during these excursions we would ride the canals of Amsterdam, but my favorite place to go was Volgendam. To get there dad and I would go across the Ijssel Meer on a small boat. Here the villagers still wore their 17th century Dutch boeren clothing. They looked very picturesque in their outfits and marvelous hats along with their wooden shoes. Throughout the village there were colorful houses painted in pink, green, and orange, each with its own unique 17th century style architecture.

While in Volgendam, we would eat salted herring with chopped onions for lunch, along with a piece of bread. Sometimes I would get treated to spek koek or an olie boll for desert. Mom still cooked Indonesian food at home. I tried some of the Dutch dishes that she made, but potatoes and spinach were not my favorite things to eat. Maybe I was too spoiled from eating spicy food with a lot of herbs. Here at Volgendam the seafood was more to my liking.

My favorite trips with dad were the ones to Mastbos, in Breda, and the old remnants of World War II bunkers. Mastbos when I was young was a huge forest, dark and mysterious with all sorts of creatures and evildoers roaming within its confines. It was my own Sherwood Forest, and I loved spending time there with dad.

At eight years old I didn't have much of an allowance. With a growing family, I don't think mom and dad had too much left over to give out on allowances. It was during this time that my younger brother Albert was born. He was probably named after dad. So with my sisters, Connie, Sylvia, Ingrid, and my brother Louie all vying for their share of the allowances, I decided to get a job.

The only job I could get was working for the fodder man. He was the person who would go down our neighborhood streets and pick up the garbage. With his horse drawn cart, we would pick up all that was piled on the street early in the morning around 6 am. Most of the garbage was left over food items like rotting meat and vegetables. When the day's work was done we would go to his farm and it became my job to haul the stuff to the pigpens and feed the pigs. For this smelly and undignified job he paid me fifty cents a week, but he would also give me all the milk and cheese I wanted.

As the years went by, I became more aware of the events that were going on around my life. The apartheid that I experienced in Indonesia now became apparent to me. This time; however, I was on the receiving side. The world became a nastier place to live in. Although they were what now seem inconsequential events, at that time when I was eight and nine years of age they were life-changing moments.

Apart from the usual name-calling and physical harassment by the Kaaskops, white Dutch boys, there were events on our street, the river by my Oom Ed's house in Amsterdam, and on television that would alter my way of looking at the world. I had arrived at the age of enlightenment and would become more cynical, and hardened, as the years passed by.

On Heemskerk Straat lived a family with twin boys. They were the typical Dutch kids who kept to themselves and weren't troublemakers. I didn't really play with them much, but I think my sister Connie knew them more than I did. Most of the time coming home from school I would walk past their house, there was always some commotion going on inside their place. Sometimes one of the twins would dart out the front door dressed like a girl. I never thought anything of it especially at nine years old. As time went by, the story was that his parents wanted a girl and they treated him as one. Whether there is any truth to this story or not, he ended up thinking of himself as a girl and became one. After awhile I never saw him again. Even at that age I felt sad for the kid.

Oom Ed lived in Amsterdam, by a nice river. When we came to visit him, I would always go fishing. I went by myself. My fishing gear consisted of a cane pole with some string and a homemade hook made from a safety pin. I bought the cane pole and some worms at the little fishing store in town.

One day I was happily fishing alongside the banks of the river. It was overcast with small breaks of sunshine shining through. I had no worms so I made some bait using bread dough. It worked beautifully and I had a pail full of pan fish in no time. So here I was enjoying this wonderful day until the Kaaskops came. They were young teenagers bent on causing trouble, and I became their hapless victim. Beaten up and humiliated by their verbal abuse of my ethnicity, they kicked over my pail of fish as a final insult. Scrambling towards the river I managed to save some of my fish. Angered by the event, I went home to Oom Ed's place and told him what happened. He wasn't much help. I would make it a point to learn judo from then on. Nothing happened with learning the finer art of fighting until I went into the military. I did, however, become more aware of the prejudice that went on around me.

I always looked forward to visiting Oom Ed and Tante Jane; they were the only people I knew that had a television set in their house. In those days there was only one channel and they always showed the news. Occasionally they would show a World War II documentary about the German occupancy. It was very disturbing to me. One night as we sat in front of the television they showed the beginnings of the Berlin wall being put up by the Russians. The street scenes were chaotic. People were running through barbed wire barricades on rain-soaked streets trying to get to freedom. Shots were heard, and in the following weeks the progress of that wall was shown nightly. I was beginning to harden towards the communist, because now I was looking at other people losing their freedom and homes like I did in Indonesia. In my young mind the seeds of war was being fostered. It would be years later after my time of active service with the US Navy, and during Ronald Reagan's presidency that I would see that Berlin Wall come down, but by then I was a cynical, hardened, and insensitive man.

Breda, Holland, was beginning to wear me down. The weather was miserable during the time that we lived there. Sunshine was missing most of the year and it became tiresome to me. I probably can assume correctly that it had the same effect on my sisters Connie, Sylvia, Ingrid, and brothers Louie, and Albert, not to mention my mom.

Mom was always busy with the house and the kids. Sometimes it would overwhelm her, and dad would send us off to stay at my oom's house or with other relatives. During one of these stays at someone else's house I got into a fight with their obnoxious son, and after being chastised by his equally obnoxious father, I ran away. After being gone for most of the day I went back. Somehow dad heard about it and we were never sent to live somewhere else.

Throughout the years that I lived in Breda, not much changed in my uneventful miserable existence. Except for the time when I went to the downtown area of Breda where I forgot that I had my brother Louie with me and lost him, and when I got hit by a motorbike while trying to cross the street, life went on as usual. Little did I know that dad was planning to go to America. So on a cold wintry day mom and dad packed up the family, we boarded a KLM airplane at Shiphol Airport, and flew off for New York, USA. My gray wintry days of life in Breda, Holland, had come to an end, and I was headed for a land filled with sunshine and promise.

L to r, front to back: Edward, Louie, Albert, Roy, Connie, Sylvia, and Ingrid in the 1960s, Pasadena, California, before Leslie was born.

Oma (Moes) Emma Grillet, Van Westbroek. Dad's mom

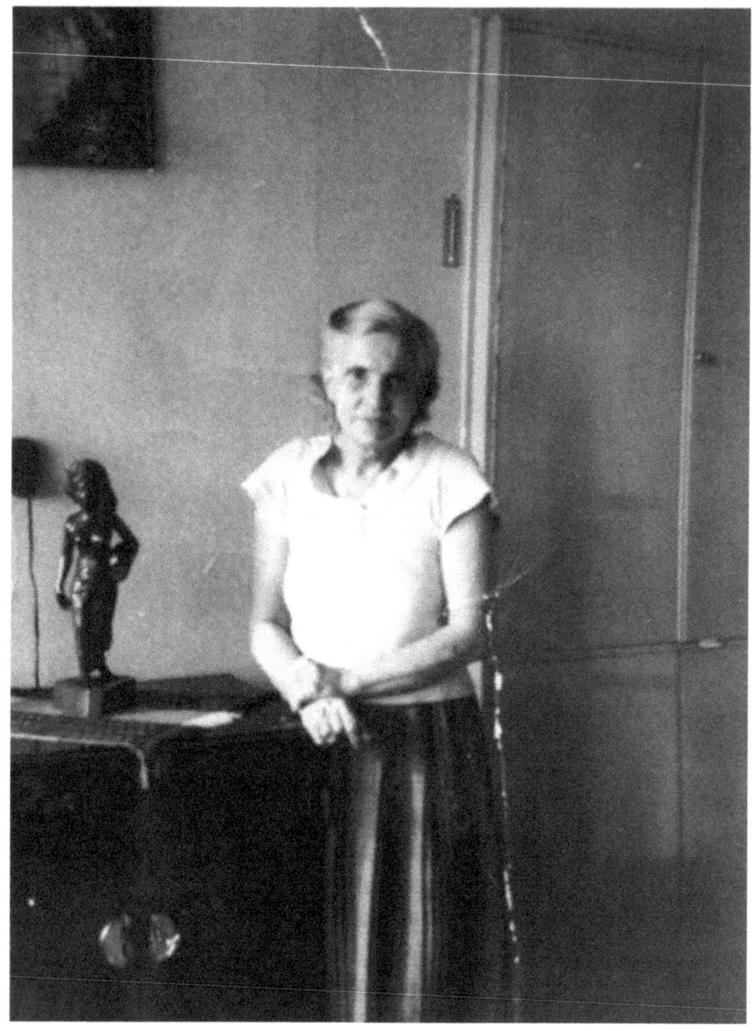

Oma Rotschke Van Gemert. Mom's mother

Connie, Roy, Sylvia, Ingrid, and Louie in the back yard on 46 Heemskerk Straat in Breda, Holland

Dad and Roy in Mastbos, Breda, Holland

Efteling a fantasy park of story books like Hansel and Gretel

The magical Arabian Castle in Efteling Park, Breda, Holland

4

Good Old America

Man we are going on an airplane from Shiphol, Holland, to the USA, it wasn't going to be as exciting as traveling on a ship, but at least it was going to be faster. This was the first time I had ever been on an airplane, and I was really curious about the planes cockpit and the crew. Of course I didn't get to sit by a window seat, but it didn't really matter much. So here I went with visions of cowboys and Indians in my head. Which is what I believed America was all about. I had it in my mind that in America everyone was rich. So there I was flying away to my new country not knowing how disillusioned I was about America.

Finally we arrived at New York's airport, I don't recall what the weather was like, and all I knew was that New York was big and crowded. New York's skyline was filled with tall skyscrapers that seemed to reach forever into space. The street scene was one of chaos, cars, and people everywhere. It was noisy and smelled of gasoline and trash, not clean and quiet like Breda, Holland. Dad took us to a hotel near Rockefeller Square. I could see an ice-skating rink from our window. It was amazing. We stayed here a couple of days; I guess dad was waiting to get things organized with our American sponsor. We didn't get to go out much into the street, which was ok by me. The city was not what I had expected and it was overwhelming. New York City was alien to me.

Finally, after a few days, dad got us off to the train station. We would be on the train for four days and three nights, and go from New York City all the way to California. I had visions of buffaloes, cowboys, and Indians dancing in my head. The train we took was named the Santa Fe Super Chief and it was huge, and beautiful. The conductors were black, and for the first time in my life I have seen a real black man. I was eleven years old, and in Holland and Indonesia I always thought that black men were white men in black face paint. It sure was interesting.

Boarding the train, I hurriedly ran for a window seat and found one. The train hissed, and while belching smoke it slowly started to roll down the tracks. We rode the rails for miles on end, the soothing chucking sound of the engine and wheels settling me into a state of serenity and calmness. I had my nose plastered to the window. This can't be true; I saw broken down shacks and cars; houses with broken TV antennas slowly deteriorating with their peeling paint and broken windows sitting in yards that had weeds and were devoid of grass. America had poor people? This was not the America I had come to believe in.

The Santa Fe Super Chief made a lot of stops in all the different states. We couldn't go outside the train, so we watched the passengers come and go. Here were people of different nationalities and financial status; most were middle class, some were poor; not the rich that I had believed all Americans were. Traveling through to the West, I never saw the cowboys and Indians that I thought I would see in America. They only existed in the few movies that I saw in my youth living in Holland.

There was one thing that didn't disappoint me. It was the beautiful landscapes that went by my private window in America. Golden fields filled with miles of wheat, corn, and barley. Farms so big that they stretched beyond the horizon filled with farm animals. I saw the prairies with their antelope, deer, and birds of all kinds, but no buffalo. Horses were seen too, but few cowboys, and hardly any Indians riding them.

Riding through the Midwest, the landscape turned into a desert region filled with orange-red canyons, and mountains. This must have been parts of Texas, New Mexico, and Arizona. I was too young to really know. I was in wonder of all the places that I saw. This was not Holland, and I was no longer disillusioned by my youthful belief of what America was.

After four days and three nights we reached California; at least here there were palm trees and lots of greenery, after we had passed through the desert.

California, the land of milk, honey, and movie stars; I would see movie stars everywhere, but I didn't. The train rolled through Duarte, Monrovia, Arcadia, and stopped in Pasadena. The cities didn't stand out in my mind, but Pasadena would make an impression on mom. We finally reached Union Station in downtown Los Angeles, where we would stop and meet our sponsor. It was a fantastic station with murals and décor that I was very impressed with.

Los Angeles was like New York City, except for the lack of skyscrapers. The tallest building that I saw was city hall, but I wouldn't know this until my later years. Across the street from the station was a Mexican village; later I would learn that this was Olvera Street. After dad and mom got our luggage and met the sponsor, we set off for our new home. The drive in the car was great; it was the first time that I had ever been in a car.

The car pulled over in front of an apartment complex that was located across the street from MacArthur Park in Los Angeles. It was huge. Inside the building were several rooms; dad and mom would have one room; five kids shared the other one. We also shared a communal bathroom. I'm not sure why we were only assigned two bedrooms for the whole family. I was just happy that we had arrived. It had been a long and tiring trip.

One of my most memorable memories concerned shopping for the first time in Los Angeles. Mom needed some cleaning supplies, and she asked Connie and I to go next door to the small grocery store on 6th Street. Well we were glad to go, but there was one problem, we didn't know any English except for yes and no. So off we went to buy some Vim, a powdered cleaning product. It was hilarious. The storeowner asked what we wanted and through hand gestures and laughs we finally got some Ajax cleanser. He knew Spanish, but no Dutch.

My first taste of eating a sandwich was horrible. I wasn't used to the food here in America, it had too many preservatives, and I could taste it in everything I ate. I had a peanut butter sandwich made with white bread and Peter Pan peanut butter. I threw it away. Where was the Indo or at least the Dutch food? Well the fruits were good.

6th Street was a wide street, nothing like the small cobblestone streets in Holland, and crossing it would be a challenge for the first few times. Every minute of the day a police car or ambulance would go by with sirens blaring. It was stressful to say the least. It was noisy all the time.

There were a lot of stores on 6th Street. People would shop and scurry about. Some went to the movie theater, but most went to MacArthur Park. The park had a small lake with boats that you could rent. It also had a lot of trees, and a stage where a band could perform. There were also a lot of pigeons flying around and pooping on everything and everybody. So after crossing that danger filled 6th Street, I found my solace in the park.

MacArthur Park was my favorite place to go after school. Most of the time I would sit in my favorite tree and watch the cars going by. On the lake there were couples necking, and others trying to catch fish. I don't think it even had fish. There were all sorts of people that were in the park; a lot of them seemed strange to me. The language they spoke was foreign, and I didn't understand a word that was being spoken.

During the weekends there were soccer games, and I got to play a few of them. The soccer players knew I could play and that I was from Holland. Most were Mexican or Latin American and spoke broken English, so I fit right in. They showed me how to catch the pigeons incase I wanted to eat them. A string with a big loop would be thrown on the pathway, and some breadcrumbs or corn would be thrown in the middle of the loop. So we sat there and watched them hover around in a circle before they landed inside the loop, a quick jerk and you had dinner. I didn't know at that age that squab was a delicacy, so I gave mine away. I learned a lot from the people I met in MacArthur Park in Los Angeles.

Learning English became dad's and mom's first priority for my sisters, my brothers, and myself. They forbade us to speak

Dutch in the house. The culprit who was caught would have a bar of soap stuck into their mouth. Well, maybe I'm exaggerating. Television would have to be given credit for us learning the English language. We didn't have a TV, so we went into the parking lot behind the apartment and watched through our neighbor's window. They knew us, and they left their blinds open. I would have to say that I learned a lot of English from watching cartoons and the Three Stooges. In those days TV only came on for a few hours, and on a daily basis I would watch Sheriff John at noon. I loved the red light green light episodes. Milk anyone? It would take mom a long time to learn English.

School had its own particular problems. The first school I went to was Commonwealth Elementary in Los Angeles. It was strange. They didn't have teachers who knew how to speak Dutch, and they didn't have a bilingual program for us. So there I was in school outdoing everyone in math and geography and not having a clue about spelling and phonics. My first word the teacher had me spell was potato. I almost got it right. Slowly but surely I became proficient with English by the age of fourteen, with an accent of course. Throughout my growing years, I bounced through several schools.

My most challenging school was in South Central LA. After a few months dad had gotten a better job and moved the family to Menlo and 66th Street to a single home. The neighborhood had been a Jewish community, that's what I have been told, and they were leaving. The block I lived in had a lot of black boys. My first day of school was interesting. I was in the fifth grade; didn't speak English too well, and my clothes were different. They had a field day with me.

One particular black kid had it in for me. He would lie in wait in the morning and after school to catch me, and try to beat me up. He had friends to help him; I had nobody. So it became a daily ritual to run to school and back. They caught me a couple of times. Connie would try to help me when she could.

I did get back at the black kid one day. Apparently he was in trouble over something, and he came running up the stairs to our house to seek shelter. Louie and I got a hold of a broom handle and pushed the smuck down the stairs. Connie helped him and hid him under the sink. He was shaking and scared. I still don't know why, but I felt bad for him. He never did bother me again after that. I saw a couple of bruises on his albino face. He probably had his challenges too, like I had mine on Menlo Street in Los Angeles.

We finally left Menlo Street and moved to Huntington Beach where dad was going to buy a house. For some reason he was never able to buy the place. So after a few months we left for Pasadena, California. We moved to Vista Avenue in the neighborhood bordered by Foothill Boulevard and Sierra Madre

Villa. It was a nice place and dad had gotten rid of his old clunker Dodge and got a Chevy Belair. He was moving up the ladder in his work and became more successful financially. His English became better. I think he went to college to get his existing college degree that he had from Holland recognized and certified. So he got a bigger and better car for himself and the family.

I have great memories of driving in dad's cars. The one I enjoyed the most was when he would pack all of us in his black 1948 Dodge and head for the beach. I can relate to the stories about Mexican families and packing their cars full of people. One day when we were going on our beach trip, he was driving down a hill and had to stop really fast; well his brakes failed and he hit the car in front of him. The two guys in the car made a big fuss and told him they were going to sue him. I didn't happen, they were ex felons and probably couldn't sue dad; at least that's what the cops told him. After this minor mishap we headed for the beach. It was probably Redondo Beach. In Holland we hardly ever went to the beach. I had a great time especially when it came time for lunch, we had fried chicken, something too expensive in Holland, and all the trimmings. The car trips were great including the trips to Las Vegas, and Sequoia National Park.

So it was in Pasadena, California, that our lot improved. I would be going to Marshall Junior High School, and then Blair High School where I would meet many of my friends that I would grow up with and experience the turbulent Sixties. It was a place where I would become more frustrated, and bitter, along with learning the English language.

The first thing I noticed about Pasadena was the mountains and the palm trees; they were beautiful. Our neighborhood was pretty quiet, and it was located about half a block away from the Pasadena Rose Parade route. Next door to us was another Dutch Indonesian family and they had a couple of kids. Being new on the street I had no friends; I usually played with my sisters and brothers which to me was pretty cool; we were pretty close after all the relocation we had endured. A few weeks later I met my first friends in America, a couple of boys who lived down the block from us behind the Klokes liquor store on Sierra Madre Villa Blvd. They were Navajos, Wesley and Brian. Later on in school I would meet more Indo boys at Marshall Jr. High.

School started in September 1962, and I would be in the seventh grade going to Marshall Jr. High School. Connie and I had to walk about four miles to get there; I don't think there was any busing going on in the Pasadena School District. The weirdness of going to a new school didn't faze me much after having been bounced from school to school a lot in the last year. At least this school was located in a great area, not the slums of Los Angeles. Marshall was big compared to the other LA schools

I had gone to. It also had some beautiful landscaping and great athletic fields. So off I went to register.

The registration office was crowded with new students, so I waited my turn. I surveyed the room and found that the majority of the students and staff were white. Kind of strange to me, I was used to seeing more of a mixture since that's all I was exposed to in my other schools. I don't think there were any more than two-dozen or so Negroes, Mexicans, Asians, or Indo's in the entire school; this made me a special student. When my turn came, I was asked what my goals were for school. Hell I didn't know. I had been bounced around so much that I didn't give it much thought. So I told them that I wanted to be in the Merchant Marine as a deck officer. The lady looked surprised, and said I would have to take college prep classes, which was fine with me. She must have been intrigued by my answer. With schedule in hand, I went to my classes; instead of the usual rowdiness in the classroom, I found well-mannered students and pleasant teachers. In one of my classes, I believe reading; I met Alfred, another Indo from Holland. We would have some great times growing up in Pasadena at his house with his brothers and neighbors.

The one thing I liked about California schools was the three-month summer break that was in the yearly schedule. In Holland we only had a month break from school. So the summer was long and hot with a lot of time to do whatever I wanted; most of the time I hung around with my sisters and brothers. Dad and mom would take us on trips to the beach and Sequoia National Park.

At last summer was over, and I went back to school at Marshall. Great, at least I was going back to the same school for once. I met with Alfred, who told me he had met another Indo boy from Holland, and asked me if I wanted to meet him. Sure why not, I had nothing to lose. As we crossed the walkway on the second floor to another building, Alfred spotted him and introduced us to each other. His name was Bill. I couldn't believe it, two kids from the same place I came from, with the same story of being relocated from our homeland. Somehow my loneliness had begun to ebb; here were two people who could relate to what I had been experiencing in my life since leaving Indonesia; I clung on to their friendship for dear life. Bill would become my best friend, and still is today. I consider him my brother. Bill, his dad Harry, and I, would have some great times going hunting together. I would also mourn with Bill the times of his family's tragedies.

I wasn't much of a troublemaker at Marshall. I spent my time trying to pass my classes. The majority of classes prepared me for the SAT tests so I could go on to college later on. My favorite class was gym class. One day in the school's main office I came across the school's yearbook. I kept noticing certain students were in all of the group pictures. I had an idea that if I joined the football, baseball, and track teams, I too could be in the pictures. So I signed up for baseball. It was a total comical farce. Sure I could play baseball with my friends at Jefferson Park on Villa Street, but school baseball?

Things didn't start off right from the beginning. The baseball uniform the coach gave me was too big, and it made me look like a dork. Most of the players had played in Little League Baseball, so they had an edge, as it turned out I was a better player. Bored with the facade of being a sports jock, I quit the team as soon as the team's picture was taken. I would become like the rest of the picture glory hogs.

Confident in my ability to fool the staff, I tried to get away with a few more ideas that I had. It was not to be, somehow Alfred, Bill, and I got into some trouble, and we were called into the office. I can't even remember what we did. For punishment, Mr. Kraft, who was in charge of school security, railroaded us into becoming school safety officers, badge and all. I thought it was hilarious; it's like putting the fox in the hen house. There are of course many humorous stories concerning our stint as security officers at Marshall. Well, at least I got into another group picture in the yearbook

Times spent at Marshall Jr. were great with some special memories. Each month the air raid siren across the street would sound off, and we would have to duck and cover in our classroom. I found it amazing that this procedure would save us from annihilation in a nuclear attack. As a naughty teenager, I found it fantastic, since I could check out the beaver shots from the girls under the student desks in front of me.

After graduating in June 1965, from the ninth grade at Marshal Jr. High School, I was sent to Blair High School, the new school that the Pasadena School District had built. It was about ten miles from our new house on Michigan Avenue, located west of Hill Street and bordered by Villa Street on the south and Orange Grove Blvd. to the north.

Dad bought the house in 1963, and it was a great accomplishment for him. I'm totally impressed by this as I look back on it today. Here was a man with broken English skills, a family of eight, and barely three years since his immigration to America accomplishing the American dream of buying a house.

Michigan Avenue had a canopy of trees covering it. It was a neighborhood whose residents were mostly white families. We could be considered the first block busting family on the block, and I would have some great memories of this. The house had belonged to an actor Mr. Bradley. To our right as you look from the street we had Mrs. Jansen, a Dutch lady, and to our left was Mr. Gary, a real racist of a guy.

For some reason Mr. Gary had a dislike for the family, particularly me. He would always confront me when I was watering the front lawn as part of my chores for my allowance. He had a big beef about water flowing over the sidewalk in front of his house, not to mention the fact according to him, that I was wasting too much water on the lawn. Muttering under his breath, I could hear his vicious racial slurs about the family and me. It was war, and I was going to hound the old man to death. Every day I would go out and water the lawn for free if need be, and watch the water flow over his sidewalk. As usual he would come out, and I would enjoy seeing the blood veins in his neck pop out on his reddening face. I knew he could never win; I had learned to accept who I was and began to overcome my disillusionment of my youth. I would become a teenager, and a young adult in this house before I went off to do my service to America.

In September 1965, Bill and I set off for Blair High School. They had us bused there from Hill Street. It was weird being on a bus with all the different kids. The bus driver would always have the radio on; he liked to listen to the top ten on the radio. At that time there were only AM stations: we had KRLA, KHJ, KFWB, and radio jocks like Casey Kasem, the Real Don Steele, and

Wolfman Jack. I loved the Animals, and the Byrds. So off we went, with rock and roll surrounding us, to school on the bus.

Blair was a brand new high school, it didn't even have a dining room, so we had to go across the street to the park and have our lunch. They were still building the auditorium that was shaped like a diamond. In order to accommodate the students, they would put in bungalows for classrooms later on in the school's history. But for now the athletic fields, swimming pool, and track, were under construction.

To get to the park we had to use a tunnel where the vending machines were. On a daily basis I would run to them and get the prized hot dog with chili burrito. It was a mad dash between everyone, and too bad for the loser who got there late; it would be empty. In the park were groups of students, each within their own click: you had the Indo's: greasers, blacks, surfers, sport jocks, dopers and non-dopers, and the up and coming hippies; they were a mixture of the baby boomer generation lost in space. Times were changing in America, and it was being reflected in its youth.

In Alfred's room at the back of his house hung a poster with a soldier jumping over a log in a jungle setting, it read " Come to Vietnam for the Action" at least that's how I still remembered it. There would be a lot of heated discussions about topics concerning the draft, Vietnam, war in general, and girls. I would spend hours in his room reading his comic books, and reflecting on life in general.

Once in awhile we would cruise in his car, a small white Ford. We would cruise Colorado Blvd. in search of chicks. Colorado Blvd. was where the happening crowd would spend their days, especially around Fair Oaks Street and the LA Free Press building where the hippies would hang out on the sidewalk. It had numerous bars and eateries like Taco Ernies, Hazels Bar, The Thirty Fiver, and Barnacle Bills down the street. During the Sixties it was a run down area, Pasadena's so-called ghetto, today it's a sheik ultra modern old town Pasadena tourist trap. Driving through this area Alfred and I along with Marty would check out the scene. There was probably dope dealing going on, people yelling, and some fine hippie chicks to check out. It was everything a seventeen-year-old boy found important in his life.

Sometime during 1966 I met Dan, he lived behind Alfred's house. Dan was a struggling musician who liked the blues. He looked like Mick Jagger from the Rolling Stones. I heard him playing one day as I sat in Alfred's room, and decided to go over and check it out. Of course he was surprised to see me, and after introducing myself he let me in. I would come to embrace Dan as one of my best friends and brother. We would both come of age during the mid Sixties. I have lost touch with Dan in the last decade, but he called me when his brother Bill got a heart attack, and his other brother John passed away. I miss Dan a lot, but knowing that he is still here gives me comfort.

Right after my eighteenth birthday in 1968, I graduated from Blair High School, and spent most of my time bumming around. I knew I was going to be drafted in the near future, and had a hard time getting a real job. I went to Pasadena City College for a while, where I took writing classes, and began work in earnest to improve my skills in English grammar and usage, but got bored with it, so I left. What had started as my dad's and mom's vision of us learning English had come to fruition. I had overcome my broken English, and was dealing with my disillusion of America. I still believed she stood for equality, fairness, and Christian kindness.

Mike and Roy in Spain

5

Military Life

My time as a free man would not last long after I left Pasadena City College. When I was seventeen years old, I had a hair brain idea to join the US Army as an artilleryman in the airborne units. Dad had signed the paperwork, and I went to get my physical and passed. When the day came for me to report to the induction center he was supposed to take me, but he never did. So for the next year I went to night school, where I took some classes in order to go to Pasadena City College. I stayed at PCC until April 1969. I had already received my 1A classification from the Selective Service Agency, and it would only be a matter of time, after they found out that I had left school, that I would be drafted.

Most of my friends and acquaintances were either in Vietnam, the US Army, or Marine Corps. Some had come back from overseas, others were getting ready to go, and the neighborhood had become a quiet place. I felt bored just hanging around, and maybe had a sense of guilt for not doing my part. In May 1969, I went to the USMC recruiting station on Washington Blvd. and Lake Street in Pasadena. It was a small office with two rooms, one for the US Marines and the other the US Navy. I went inside and found the Marine Corps recruiter on the telephone, so I wandered around the room looking at all the propaganda posters. After surveying these, I went into the other room and started looking at the US Navy posters. The US Navy recruiter asked if he could help me, I said no, I was waiting for the Marine Corps recruiter.

Petty officer Washington was a very convincing recruiter, he gave me valid reasons why I should join the US Navy, which I did. Needless to say the Marine Corps recruiter was upset when he came into the US Navy's office and learned what had happened. I was to report to the induction center within a couple of weeks, but I asked if we could postpone it to early June. I had some things that needed to be done.

June 3, 1969, was to change my life forever; my sister Sylvia and her husband Don took me to the induction center on Figueroa Street near 7th Street in downtown LA. It was early in the morning around 5 am. The ride was pretty quiet, not much talk going on. Don had served in the US Army a year ago, so he knew what it was all about. When we arrived at the center there were protesters outside on the sidewalk and by the entrance to the building. Sylvia and Don dropped me off, said their goodbyes, and left.

It took me a minute to get my bearings and to calm myself before I went in. Before I reached the door, I saw a couple of men walk up to me. They had something wrong with their arms and neck. When they came closer I saw that they had horrific wounds from napalm, a gasoline jelly substance used to burn out the enemy. Both had been in the Marine Corps, and received their wounds in Vietnam. The skin on their arms and neck looked like it had been peeled back, exposing the bluish blood veins on their brownish red burned skin. I felt embarrassed looking at them. When they asked if I got drafted, I said no, I had enlisted in the US Navy, they wished me luck.

Entering the building, I found it crowded with men. I checked in at the desk and was told to follow the red line. The whole floor had red, yellow, and blue lines, running all over the place to the testing stations. So unless you wanted to screw with the induction center staff, it was pretty hard to get lost. It took about two hours to go through all the stations. There were some memorable moments from that time.

The one that stands out the most was when we were made to stand naked waiting to go into one of the stations. I don't know why we had to do this, but standing next to me was a pygmy sized black man, about five feet tall, with an extremely large private section; think elephant. I don't know how he felt, but I was totally embarrassed. Everyone in the room was focused on him, and since I was standing next to him, I was in everyone's point of view also. I believe everyone within two feet of the guy probably felt the same way I did.

Finally I had finished checking in, and all that was left was taking the oath, they had us line up on both sides of the hallway. There were probably about a hundred and fifty of us, and here comes a Marine Corps sergeant who yelled at us to pay attention. With a stern voice he asked where the draftees were, to those who raised their hands he made an announcement not to move from their place in line, and that every third man was to be drafted into the Marine Corps. You could hear a pin drop; I might even have heard a whimper, but nobody moved.

They took us into a large room with flags, banners, and a picture of President Johnson on the walls. This is where they gave us a speech on how proud they were about us, and gave us the oath of allegiance to the United States. After that they herded us to the sixth floor where I would spend the rest of the day until around five o'clock. For lunch they marched us down Figueroa Street to The Pantry Cafe for two brown bag lunches, which consisted of a couple of sandwiches; fruit; chips; and a boxed drink. One we were to eat at the center, the other was for the bus trip to boot camp.

The time spent waiting to go on the buses was boring, except for the near fights when someone tried to cheat at cards, or the throwing of the dice. As is always the case, people congregate to those that have similar upbringing or personalities. I met a guy who was brought up in a Marine Corps family, and of course he was going to be a US Marine. Six o'clock came and they had us walk up four blocks to the greyhound bus station. I boarded the bus; my great US Navy adventure had started.

After a few hours on the bus we finally pulled in to the bus station in downtown San Diego. We were told not to wander off, so we just milled around. In a couple of minutes the gray US Navy bus pulled up, and I got on board with mostly Marine Corps recruits and a dozen or so US Navy recruits. It was pretty somber on the bus with everyone craning their necks to see glimpses of San Diego. The bus went through a small tunnel and entered the MCRD, (Marine Corps Recruit Depot), stopped at the guardhouse, and was told to park a few feet away from it. Immediately after the bus door opened a screaming Marine Corps drill instructor came aboard, and told all the Marine Corps recruits to get the hell off the bus and form up on the shoe marks. He told the rest of us girls to stay on the bus. I had an insane urge to laugh, but I knew better not to. I could just see and smell the fear on those Marine Corps recruits, and I initially wanted to be one of them, thank God for small miracles and the US Navy recruiter. I had been saved from the Marine Corps.

The bus left the MCRD and a sigh of relief could be heard from every sailor onboard. It would only take about fifteen minutes before we reached the Naval Training Center in San Diego. Most of the buildings were painted battleship gray. The bus pulled in around sunset, and it was starting to get dark when it finally arrived at the building where I would be assigned my training company. Exhausted from the day's events I was told to get a bunk inside for the night. I'm sure the rest of the recruits were as happy as I was.

My first night in the US Navy will always be my most memorable event during my entire service career. Whenever I feel down or blue I like to think back on this moment. While resting on my bunk, I would hear "Taps" for the first time; it brought a chill and a sense of foreboding and loneliness the likes of which I have never felt. In the silence of the barracks amid the dark shadows, I could hear men softly whimper and call out for their mom. It must have been their first time away from home. Outside, near the window I was sleeping by, I heard a couple of happy sailors walk by, laughing hysterically one of them kicked a can and exclaimed jubilantly that tonight was his last night in the US Navy after four years of service. It would be a long time in a place far away that I would make that same statement myself, but at that moment I felt lost.

A loud noise like a can being trashed around the room woke me up. It was still dark outside. Some sailor was running from bunk to bunk waking everyone up, told us to get ready, and be outside by 4:30 am. The madness had begun. After breakfast we came back to the same barracks and were told to line up on the footprints. We stood around for about five minutes and were greeted by a US Navy chief dressed in his khakis, and a young sailor in his blues. The chief told us that he was Machinist Mate Chief Wilhoit; I had no idea what he was talking about. Since we had shown up late at the NTC, he was to be our company commander for our new company, NTC Recruit Company 403, something he didn't appreciate, and would make us bear the wrath of his disappointment in missing out on the company he wanted.

Chief Wilhoit was a complex man, he had a gimpy left arm, and projected an image of kindness and caring, but it was just a ruse to get you off guard. I would always get my kicks watching his face turn red when someone screwed up. As always, he would get a chokehold around the hapless recruit and bully him against the wall with his face inches away yelling at the poor soul. I never gave him any reason to do that to me.

The training at NTC lasted nine weeks, learning about US Navy customs, shipboard procedures, the tear gas chamber, marksmanship, and survival skills like swimming and staying afloat at sea. Recruits in the company that I was in were mostly from California, and we never won any of the competition banners. Most of us just wanted to finish boot camp with the minimal effort required, and move on to school and sea duty. Of course we had our man in the company that could never get things right, he became Chief Wilhoit's main focus to direct his frustration on for one reason or another. The kid was trying his best, but he was just awkward, and didn't seem too intelligent or street savvy. He probably grew up in a very small town, or the boonies. Here was a guy who wanted to be a sailor, and was being tormented by his superiors. Near the end of boot camp they slacked off on him; he graduated with our company and was assigned to a minesweeper headed for Vietnam. I feel bad sometimes, because I don't remember his name, or if he came home alive and well.

Two weeks into my training our company was standing in morning formation to go to breakfast, Chief Wilhoit came out with a devious smile on his face and informed ten of us, including myself, that we had been drafted. I thought he was joking. Since he was so disappointed in us, he saw no reason not to get us out of his US Navy. With a leering voice he pointed towards the MCRD's running track, which was adjacent to our base, and stated that most if not all of us would be sent to the Marine Corps. For some reason I didn't believe him, and when it was my turn to choose what I wanted to do, I told him I loved the US Navy, and to tell the draft board that I was staying.

Would he please send the telegram to my mom? There were two that wanted to leave and go into the US Army: one that went next door to the Marine Corps, seven of us stayed, and I had figured out what made Chief Wilhoit happy; he loved the USN.

During our training in boot camp, they tested us in order to place us in a job that we could excel in. My choice was to go into the Seabees and become a heavy equipment operator. The US Navy had other ideas and put me into naval aviation as an AMH (Aviation Mechanic Hydraulics); it would be something they would do during my entire active duty stint, giving me what I didn't want.

I graduated from US Navy boot camp in the early part of August 1969, and received orders for aviation school in Millington, Tennessee. After our recruit company's graduation ceremony we were able to visit with our families. Dad, mom, and my sisters and brothers were there, and I was happy to see them. I introduced Chief Wilhoit to my dad. I would never see the chief again after boot camp, but I will always remember him.

I left for Millington, Tennessee, shortly after my leave, to go to aviation school. I had visited Alfred's mom and dad to see how things were going with him in Vietnam, they seemed worried but said he was fine, little did I know that their other son Steve had plans to volunteer for the draft, and would probably head for Vietnam too. They wished me well when I left. The neighborhood had changed. No one was home anymore. My friends were all in the service, and there was no reason for me to hang around, so I left to do my duty to my country.

During 1969 the war was being protested on a daily basis. I was naïve and proud enough to still wear my US Navy uniform, full dress blues, to the airport in Los Angeles. I was heckled and ridiculed even though I was not wearing the Vietnam Service ribbons, the protesters didn't care, and I was an easily identifiable target.

Duty at the Naval Aviation Training Center in Millington, Tennessee, was great. It was about a ten-week program that taught me the basics of aircraft mechanics and hydraulics. I was enthusiastic from the moment I arrived, and excelled in my studies. During the weekends we would get liberty, and I headed for Memphis with a couple of my friends. I was nineteen years old and couldn't buy any alcohol; my US Navy identification card stated this. I was going to take full advantage of my reward for being such an outstanding student. The other students had to study and couldn't leave the base.

Memphis was awesome. I had heard about the city being famous for the blues. So when we got there I checked out some of the clubs, but couldn't stay because I wasn't allowed to drink. Well, I ended up going to the amusement park and rode the merry go round and checked out the barbeque and hamburger joints. Somehow we ended up on a rural road heading out of Memphis. I still can't remember to this day why we went. We tried hitchhiking, but nobody would pick us up. Somewhere on that road we came to Elvis' Graceland, the white wrought iron fence showed signs of rust and neglect, the landscaping had browned, and was withering away. I was not impressed by the place.

My time after training during the week was spent at the enlisted men's club. There I would meet the WAVES that came to dance and drink. I could usually get a beer from the bartenders, and wandered over to them. They would always ask me where I came from, and instinctively I would answer California. That wasn't the answer the girls wanted; apparently they had made a bet of some sort concerning me. So realizing what they wanted to know, I would tell them that I was Dutch and born in Indonesia. This would set off a conversation of disbelief, until I spoke to them in Dutch. Most of them probably never even heard of Indonesia and the influence the Dutch had over there. I would always get to dance with them afterwards, which pissed off the good old boys.

Our training class was informed one day that we had to attend a freedom rally and show at the civic center in Memphis. We were to standby as riot control officers because they were expecting a large crowd of protesters. So, dressed in our riot gear we were loaded on the blue US Navy buses, and went to Memphis. We were seated in the top rows away from everyone else, in case we had to make a quick exit to confront the rioters and protesters. Watching the patriotic shows was enough to make me want to gag. The protesters never did show up; rumor had it they just wanted great attendance.

I graduated from aviation school in November 1969, and received orders to go to VT-27, a training squadron, in Corpus Christi, Texas. What happened to the carrier off the coast of Vietnam, in the South China Sea, that I wanted? The training staff assured us that the top ten students would be given their choice of duty stations, and I happened to be one of them. It didn't happen. So I went home to Pasadena, California, to go on leave. I wore my US Navy dress blues to the airport, luckily for me there were no protesters at the Memphis Airport. It was a different story at LAX. After that event, I would rarely wear my uniforms until the day I retired from military service. Vietnam was becoming a thorn in the side of American society, and I was stuck in the states headed for a training squadron in Texas.

I would leave for Texas in my civvies, and avoid the demonstrators at the airport in LA. Most of the servicemen I knew had started doing the same thing, it was worth the hassle we got from our commands in order to avoid the name calling and spitting. Some of us had even bought a slightly long hair wig to wear. The wigs became part of a disguise for the veterans that I knew during the Vietnam War era who were on active duty, or in the reserves. I became more discouraged and insentive towards America, and the Vietnam War.

After landing at the Dallas-Fort Worth Airport, I changed into my blues, and boarded a small plane for Corpus Christi, where I took a cab to the naval air station. The ride was interesting and informative. The cab driver was a retired sailor who gave me useful information on where and what to do around Corpus and Texas in general. I didn't see any protester while in Texas.

The cabbie dropped me off at the squadron's hangars, a big VT-27 squadron insignia was painted on the building's façade. It was great, but it wasn't a great big beautiful aircraft carrier. An airman showed me where the personnel office was, and I checked into the unit. Once checked in, another airman boarded me on the squadron's bus and dropped me off at the barracks, where I would spend the next two years. It was an old World War II barracks, still useful for housing lower ranked enlisted personnel. It had no air-conditioning, and there were four men to a room, unless you found a way to get into a two-man room, or better yet, finagle yourself into a one-man room. In due time, I would accomplish both.

It didn't take me long to find out where the women's barracks was located; they were several yards behind the men's. I would meet some wonderful women sailors that lived there. For the next two years we would go dancing; drinking at the club; watching movies at the theater; surviving a hurricane; and sitting out the Vietnam War. My hopes of feats of heroism, and becoming a combat veteran were dashed, and put on hold here in Texas.

My first duties at VT-27 consisted of making coffee in the chief's mess, and handing out paychecks to the squadron's personnel. It was important stuff for a young airman like me. I was still nineteen years old and so naive. I had come out of aviation school as an AMHAA, (E-2) with a designated striker as an aircraft hydraulic mechanic, the job I was given belonged to a recruit fresh out of basic with no schooling.

What a bummer it was and so demeaning, until I found out what the benefits of the job were. I became proficient at doing my work and could complete it in several hours, after that I was on my own; free to do what I wanted with the rest of my time. My hours were 4:30 am to 11:30 with time off for lunch. After a few weeks, I would be heading for lunch at 9:30 and then the barracks. The coffee fund made a huge profit, since I didn't skim off the top like the previous airman did who had the job. This impressed the chiefs so much that they recommended me for an early promotion to AMHAN (E-3). They would also help me get my practical factors completed in order to qualify for the AMHAN test; this would be during working hours. I made AMHAN in less than six months, and had such excellent evaluations that the commander of the squadron wanted to recommend me for officer prep school so I could prepare for the US Naval Academy at Annapolis.

Not to be outdone with the quality of service that the chiefs were receiving, the officers had me transferred to their mess, they had their own stewards assigned to them. I was not happy; I wanted to work in my specialty and fix or fly aircraft. My cushy job in the chief's mess had ended. I complained to one of the petty officers on the flight line, and he apparently told one of the chiefs, the next day I found myself on the flight line taxiing airplanes. I would not be planning to go to naval prep school.

My remaining time spent at VT-27 was initially good. I spent most of my time working the flight line, and got promoted to AMH3 (E-4) within a year. It was 1970, and I was twenty years old. I received letters from Alfred and Steve who were still in Vietnam, and wrote them back regularly. Most of my time was spent off base in downtown Corpus Christi, where I would hang out at the marina and eat seafood in their expensive restaurants.

There was always a breeze blowing in from the gulf that kept my hair unkempt. As a petty officer third class, my financial situation had improved tremendously. I had several uncashed paychecks in my locker, and money in my savings account. The world seemed bright and beautiful. My main means of transportation to downtown Corpus Christi was the bus; it was cheap and efficient. I became friends with a guy from New York City; he loved to be dressed up in fancy suits. So the first thing we would do when we came into town was to visit his new found tailor, a short Italian man. He made wonderful dress suits, and soon I would have one of my own. I found it exciting to play the big wig in my new suit, hair slicked down and styled, while eating in fancy seafood restaurants in downtown Corpus Christi.

If I didn't go downtown, I would stay at the base and go to the movie theater. They had current flicks and showed the latest and the greatest for the price of a quarter. It couldn't be beat. One day I went and they were showing Easy Rider with Peter Fonda. I had never seen it before, and was skeptical about the quality of the movie as I entered the theater, it was virtually empty, and stayed that way through the entire picture. I decided to stay and watch the flick since I had nothing planned for the rest of the night. By the end of the movie I was furious, and had bitter feelings toward any form of redneck or persons from the South. Word of the flick got around the base somehow, and the next day it was standing room only in the theater. After that it was them or us. The power of mass media had done its job.

Well into my second year at Corpus Christi, the US Navy was starting to lose its appeal of adventure for me. It began innocently enough in 1971; I was turning twenty-one years of age and could now buy alcohol legally. So like any good airman, I began binge drinking and found myself having a great time. The duty at VT-27 was still good, and I had bought a used 1970 blue Volkswagen Beetle that got me around a lot quicker and faster. Partying could now be done off base at the local bars. Most of the bar patrons were local folks and the station personnel. They would dress up in their cowboy shirts, pants, hats, and boots. Since I've lived in Texas for two years, I had developed a taste for their clothing style and started to wear them, cowboy boots and all. By that time, I even had a Texas drawl in my speech. I looked the part, sounded the part, but my facial features could be mistaken for Oriental or Mexican, this would often land me into trouble with the boys who weren't locals. The challenge usually started over a game of pool to see who could drink their beer faster, or drink more liquor. Overtime, I became a hell of a drinker, which in turn would create problems with my work habits. My feelings towards the US Navy would become less enthusiastic.

By the time 1971 was ending, I was waiting for my rotation to sea duty, and hoping for a combat squadron in Vietnam or at least one of the aircraft carriers deployed there, hopefully the Ranger or the Kitty Hawk. I received neither one. Instead, I got extended at Corpus Christi for another six months. The duty was still good, but after close to two years it began to lose its appeal. So I kept working the graveyard shift with the flight line crew, until one day they transferred me to the airframe and paint department. I though it was a good change of pace for me since I always wanted to learn how to paint a car.

The first day at my new assignment I met the petty officer in charge, a first class metal worker. He was chewing someone out. The airmen there considered him a real redneck cracker, and he did not hide his feelings towards minority airmen. I played the game and found the work interesting, and I was getting good at it, which irritated him even more. He could find no fault with me, but he wouldn't let things go, so he got back at me with low evaluation marks. This automatically set me up for an officer review board for counseling. I still believed that America, at least in the US Navy, was fair and equitable, how wrong I was.

I went into the officer's boardroom and was interviewed by a board of four junior grade officers; they were all white. They asked me questions on my performance and behavior, and couldn't understand why my evals had dropped so significantly from my previous ones. I told them that I had been reassigned to a department that the US Navy did not train me for, and that my work there was equal to or better than the petty officers that had the training for that kind of work. I also filed a formal complaint against the petty officer in charge of the department for being discriminatory and a racist. I couldn't believe my ears when they suggested to me that a tour of sea duty would do me good. I just laughed at them and told them that was what I wanted in the first place, before they extended my tour with the squadron. I was beginning to see the utter stupidity, and good ole boy attitude that was rampant in the US Navy.

Since there wasn't a billet available for me at the squadron, they transferred me to the base itself, and I would be working at the AIMD unit. The aircraft intermediate maintenance depot was where maintenance and repair of aircraft was performed that the squadrons couldn't do due to lack of manpower skills needed to perform the work. I was elated. For once, I would be doing meaningful work that I had been trained for by the US Navy. I was assigned to the hydraulics department.

The department chief was an old salt from World War II who had close to twenty-seven years of service in. He understood my youthful exuberance, and would cut me some slack if I came to work late or with a hangover. He had assigned me to the fabrication shop where I would rebuilt aircraft brakes, manufacture new hydraulic lines, and do testing on hydraulic components to see if they were still serviceable. I loved my job, and I would make it a habit to work more hours than I needed to. My immediate supervisor became impressed with my work ethic and told the chief that I didn't need to be supervised, so I was put in charge of the shop. In addition to enjoying the work, they had moved me to the new base barracks, which had larger two men rooms with air-conditioning, a far cry from the old deteriorating barracks that the squadron had me in.

When you're assigned to the base, in addition to your regular watches you have to spend a month with the master at arms unit. They are the shore patrol and also run the base prison. When my turn came for base duty, I was given a choice of being on the shore patrol, or work in the prison and become a prisoner escort, which meant you had to accompany the prisoners when they went on their work details doing yard work at base housing, mainly officer's housing. I chose what I thought was the easiest job. After an orientation on the US Navy's prison system, and how to work and handle prisoners, I was given a prisoner escort badge. I was now empowered to make or break a prisoner's day.

My first day out of the prison compound escorting prisoners to officer's housing caught me totally off guard. Most of the prisoners were people that I knew from the squadrons that I had partied with. They were busted for being AWOL (absent without leave), or had been insubordinate to their superior officers. I was in a predicament. I still had a job to do, and thankfully they knew the jam I was in and worked diligently while they were out on the working parties. At the end of the week, they all received excellent marks on their weekly work report, which got some of them out of being in confinement, and back with the general prison population. The month's duty went by quickly, and I found myself back in the hydraulic shop.

Three days before my extension ran out, the chief called me into his office, with him was the first class petty officer that had created the mess I was in. I was told to report back to VT-27 since my orders had come in. The chief that I cared for dearly thanked me for my service to his department, and informed me that the first class petty officer was there to replace me. He caught my smile and heard me mutter what poetic justice that was. I had my sweet revenge after all. The evaluation report; however, would follow me until the end of my enlistment.

The following day I checked back into the squadron at the VT-27 personnel office. The female personnel clerk was a friend of mine, and I asked her if I got what I asked for on my dream sheet, which is a list of duty assignments that an airman asks for. She gave me a frown and said no. I had been assigned to a transport squadron in Rota, Spain, with VR-24 as a loadmaster. The US Navy in its infinite wisdom had given me a job that I was not qualified for; I was not an American citizen and couldn't get a secret clearance to perform the job, or attend loadmaster school in Texas. My chance for heroism, and combat had all but vanished when they send me to El Toro Marine Corps Base for KC-130 training. After graduation from El Toro, the US Navy finally realized their error; I was not sent to loadmaster school, but spend several weeks at home in Pasadena waiting for my orders and plane ticket to Rota, Spain.

In late February or early March of 1972, I finally received orders to VR-24 in Rota, Spain. I had just turned twenty-two years of age. I left LAX for a US Air Force base in Philadelphia; I slept most of the way there. After my arrival at the US Navy base in Philadelphia, I took a bus to the US Air Force base to catch the flight overseas. The ride was on a gloomy wet road with rain drizzling all over the place. I could see three massive smokestacks belching their smoke into a gray sky; it was utterly depressing. I didn't realize at the time that I would be returning on this same road eight months later with the Vietnam War being de-escalated and orders to go back home to California under President Nixon's early out program. I arrived at the US Air Force base and would spend two nights there waiting for the flight to take us to Spain. They had fantastic rooms for their enlisted men, and an even better club.

When the day of departure came, I was expecting a military transport plane; instead I boarded a commercial jet liner. It was a long flight to Rota, Spain. We landed mid morning at Rota, and there was a truck waiting there at the passenger terminal to take me to the squadron personnel office. I checked in with the first class personnel petty officer and was told to get a haircut, check into the barracks with my gear, take a tour of the city, and report back the next day. I was elated and knew that I would definitely enjoy my sea duty here in Rota.

The barracks where I would stay was fairly new; comparable to the one I had at the base in Corpus. The driver said I wouldn't have to stay there very long since the base commander wanted everyone to support the local economy, and encouraged the personnel stationed here to live off base. It was fine with me. I was checked in and taken to my room that I would share with three other men; it had black walls with porno pictures plastered all over the place. My bunk was in the far corner away from the windows, no one was there in the room.

I left with the driver for my tour of the city. I had met him at KC- 130 School in El Toro, California. He asked why it took me so long to get here. So I told him the US Navy had messed up, and since I couldn't attend loadmaster school I spent my time waiting at home. He told me the squadron commander wasn't going to like that, but he was away from the base anyway while flying supply missions.

The tour of downtown Rota took about half an hour. During that time I was shown at least twenty bars, several restaurants, and businesses. I was taken along the beach area, along the sea wall, and informed that the La Guardia Civil, Spain's secret police force, will shoot you if you're caught at night on the beach. That was useful information. Then came the story about the gypsy camp that they had in town, which was burned to the ground by its citizens. Several babies died in the fire. More useful information was given; the Tokyo Bar upstairs is where our squadron goes to drink, the exchange rate was sixty pesetas to a dollar, and all the bartenders were European women on a work visa waiting to nab an American serviceman to marry them and take them home. I took it all in, and spotted the motorcycle dealership across the street from the Tokyo Bar near the traffic circle. He reassured me that more information would be given to me during the squadron's happy hour at the Tokyo after work tonight. I was as happy as a lark, and knew that I would take full advantage of this assignment in Rota, Spain.

When I got back on base, I went to my room and put away my gear. I couldn't get used to the walls being painted black; it was too depressing. My bunk was thin and crappy looking so I went to the watch desk and asked for a new one. After my gear was put away I went to tour the base. The airbase at Rota was pretty spread out, there were grass fields intermingled with block type buildings and barracks. Standing out from all of this was the control tower at the air terminal right next to the runway. On the other side of the base were the squadrons, located about a mile from the terminal. The whole complex was flat; I don't recall any mountains or hills nearby. Wandering around, I found the base package store, and the navy exchange where I went to the barbershop and got my haircut. After a two-hour excursion, I came back to my room. I found my roommates waiting for me. To this day I don't remember their names, but they were younger than I was. We would bunk together for about two months, after that I moved into town and then to Chipiona where I would live in a house on a bluff overlooking the ocean.

In the morning I got myself squared away for my meeting with the squadron's skipper. I took the base bus to VR-24's hangar and checked in. It had a big squadron logo painted on the metal building. It was a cool looking logo, a black eagle holding a bomb in its red talons over flying a carrier on a field of blue, with a silver border encircling the outer edge of a large circle. Above the logo was written VR-24, and below it "The World's Biggest

Little Airline", I was totally stoked. I still have the squadron's patch somewhere in the house, but I can't find it.

It was still pretty early, so I got some coffee and found out that they served hot dogs and hamburgers by the safety equipment shop. The skipper was in his early Forties, and had been flying KC-130s for several years. He was preoccupied most of the time. When he found out that I didn't have my loadmaster certification and couldn't fly he got upset, but understood that it wasn't my fault. So he assigned me to a non-flying billet, and I would be working with the maintenance department in the hydraulic shop. I was hoping for a flying spot as an observer on the KC-130s, but it wasn't to be. The loss of flight pay would be a bummer, and I would be stuck on the base and miss out on going to Sicily and the other bases that the squadron re-supplied.

By now, I wasn't surprised of what could happen in the US Navy; I went to the hydraulic shop and met my supervisor. He asked me what I did in my last squadron that I was in, and I told him what he wanted to know. For now he would put me on the swing shift, 4:00 pm to 11:30pm, which was fine with me. I could sleep in and still get off in time to hit the bars in Rota. Most of the swing shift crew was younger than I was; this was their first assignment fresh out of boot camp or aviation school; they considered me an old salt, so I got away from doing the dirty work.

The swing shift had it made, most of the planes were out on missions and there wasn't really much to do on the planes that were in for maintenance. Our crew was tasked to fix fuel leaks on one plane, a job we split with the graveyard shift; they only had two guys working the shift, so we would take turns going into the big planes wings and spent half the time sleeping off our hangovers. The day I left Rota for home, that plane was still in the hangar; whether the fuel leaks were fixed is unknown.

With my experience at AIMD in Corpus Christi, Texas, I could have bumped someone in the other shops that were doing hydraulic component testing, but I didn't want to be stuck inside the shop in front of the testing unit all the time. I was getting bored with the swing shift and asked the chief if I could get on the day crew and work the flight line. He said he had one option for me to work during the day, and that was to go to the base AIMD. I took it.

I knew as soon as I checked in to the AIMD department that I made a wise choice. My work here was identical to the one I had at VT-27 in Texas; even better, I would be able to get my housing and meal allotments faster so that I could move off base since I wasn't assigned to a squadron. Some of my friends had their places in downtown Rota, and I moved in with them. After a few months I bought a Honda CB 500 Four as my main mode of transportation. That bike took me all over Spain.

There wasn't much to do after work, so most of the time we went to the bars in the city. With over twenty bars in less than a square mile I had my choice of places to go. The bars weren't the sleazy, smoke filled places you usually found around US Navy bases, but were comparable to the better nightclubs in the states. Most of these had ten to twelve girls working the bar who came from Europe to find a ticket to the US. Some of them like the Tokyo Bar had a small restaurant inside them with some of the best Chinese and Spanish cuisine available. I would spend a lot of time in them, and make some fond memories there.

Whenever we get a newbie on board we would indoctrinate the newcomer. Of course he would have to buy the drinks, as was standard procedure and US Navy custom. Yeah right. My favorite spoof was to take the young sailor to the Missouri Bar, located a few blocks from the slaughterhouse as you exit the base. The smell of freshly slaughtered pigs would always linger in the air as you walked past it.

To do the procedure correctly, one of my other friends would get a small can of beef stew from the vending machines in the barracks. Off we went to the Missouri Bar, it was one of the smaller places and not too popular with the squadrons. The club had four girls working there most of the time. In we go into the semi dark interior and seat ourselves in the middle of the bar. The newbie buys us drinks until we are roaring drunk. I give the signal to Jeb at which point Jeb gets up, and sneakily opens the small can of beef stew, walks over to a bar stool and feigns getting sick, pretending to puke all over the stool. Murray upon seeing this would stagger over to the bar stool and in one swoop slurp up the stew. Needless to say the girls and the newbie were horrified. After awhile we ran out of bars to pull this stunt for obvious reasons, the supply of newbies was running out, and the bars got wise to our tricks.

My favorite past time was riding the Honda in the countryside. The roads were small two-laners running through farm fields and along the coastline. I had moved to Chipiona outside of Rota, Spain. The house I rented had a Spanish family living next door. One day I saw their young son scrupulously examining my bike. So I went to his mom and asked her if it was ok to give him a ride. His eyes lit up as we mounted the Honda. We drove around the house in a football field shaped circle for about half an hour. By the time we were through, a crowd had gathered including the La Guardia Civil. After that, the families living in the neighborhood would greet me as one of the local residents. I hope that the young boy has grown up and remembers what a great time we had, and that he has positive memories of an American sailor who served in his country.

In August 1972, I was told that President Nixon was de-escalating the war in Vietnam, and was implementing a reduction in force program for the armed forces. I was told that I probably qualified for this, and I put in my request with the justification that I was going back to college. I had moved back in to Rota, and was living on a street behind the Tokyo Bar when one of the squadron's airman came over and told me that they wanted me to transfer back into VR-24, I had received my early out. I searched for a shop to crate my Honda so I could ship it home

My remaining time in Rota, Spain, was pleasant. On a daily basis more ships and sailors came into the port. The Vietnam War was winding down; Nixon had started laying mines in Hai Phong Harbor, and my friends Alfred and Steve came home safely from the war. I didn't do much work, and even got out of standing watches. I met most of the KC-130 pilots and crewmembers, but they didn't even know I was assigned to them. The chief called me into his office to try to get me to re-enlist, but I was tired of the US Navy. I said goodbye to the skipper, but he was pre-occupied.

January 20, 1973, I found myself sitting in the air terminal. I had my dress blues on for the flight home to the Philadelphia Naval Station; it was a gorgeous sunny day. With mixed feelings, I reflected on my US Navy service and the Vietnam War, my disappointment with America and its people, and how it had hardened me and made me insentive to others. My hopes for heroism, and experiencing combat would not come to fruition. I had seen the aftermath of the Vietnam War in the broken bodies of veterans coming home, and the silver coffins coming out of the large cargo holds of the giant transport planes. It was enough.

I boarded the same commercial jet liner that brought me here to Rota, but it was a happier occasion. We were told our first stop would be in Wiesbaden, Germany, for a customs inspection before flying to the states. Smuggling dope was becoming prevalent and they were trying to get some kind of control over it. So we landed at the base and they had us go into a glass structure, take all our clothes off, and bend over to show them where the sun didn't shine. After that the dogs came and sniffed our gear and us. What a despicable way to treat an American serviceman like that.

We landed at the Philadelphia Airport; it was cold, and snowing. I only had my blues on, no jacket, but I didn't care; as soon as I got off the plane I kissed the ground. We hustled to the terminal where a second-class petty officer was waiting to load us on the bus, but he needed a shot of whiskey first, I bought him one and off we went. The ride to the naval station was on the same miserable depressing route I had taken more than eight months before; the smoke stacks were still belching their obnoxious fumes. I spent two days mustering out of the US Navy. They had us bunked in the transient barracks where I tried to give away my uniforms; nobody wanted them.

When the day arrived for me to go home to California, there was no band playing, no ceremony to mark my discharge from active service, just a US Navy bus to take me to the airport. I had my civilian clothes on, boarded the plane and flew home. I landed at LAX and caught a cab to my parent's house. Dad was working, and mom was sleeping. I had come home.

For the next couple of decades, even after my retirement from the reserves, I would struggle with feelings of survival guilt. I would feel alienated from those who never served, or ran to Canada. I would go back to Pasadena City College, but it would not be the same as before. I was a free man, but in reality I was a prisoner of my increasing bitterness and disappointment with America, the land of equality and Christian love. I would continue to serve with the US Navy Reserve, the Seabees, and finally retire from the California Air National Guard. It would be a time of growth and self-realization.

6

Family and Work

Coming home to Pasadena, California, was a quiet event, I didn't tell any of my friends when I would be home since I wasn't sure myself. I would live at my parent's house until I got settled down, and completed my registration at Pasadena City College for the upcoming semester. I went to the unemployment office and applied for my benefits. They wanted me to sign up for some training programs, which I did just to avoid the hassles from them. Being home was a weird feeling. I realized I didn't have to get up in the middle of the night to stand duty watches any more. Some of my friends in Rota had written me a couple of letters, but I didn't write them back, what was the point. Having nothing to do until school started, I would spend my free time going to bars and playing pool. It was hard to get out of the habit of binge drinking that many of the sailors did when they were on liberty. So it was with me, and it would upset my mom. When my first paycheck came in I found a small apartment and moved out. School started a week later.

My curriculum at PCC was to prepare me for a job with the US Forestry Service. I took the regular core classes in order to graduate and transfer to a four year college. I kept changing majors, and by the time I graduated after two years, I had a welding certification and an Associate of Arts degree in Engineering Technology. I was still trying to figure out what I wanted to do with my life. Like most of the veterans that I met, I had issues with re-adjusting to civilian life. I would lose interest in a subject or an occupation quickly, and end up bouncing back and forth like a rubber ball. My counselor informed me that there was a new engineering program being implemented at Cal Poly, Pomona, a four-year university, that I might be interested in. It was in the field of manufacturing engineering technology. So off I went to start the program.

I enjoyed my time at Cal Poly, it was a time when the computer was in its infancy, and a lot of the students were enrolled in the computer science field. Many of the programs that I had to do for some of my classes were typed out on IBM cards, and the only decent mainframe computer available was at Cal Tech in Pasadena. For my math classes I embraced the newly developed technology, and traded in my slide rule for a new Bowmar Brain, with floating decimal, calculator, it cost me two hundred bucks. It was incredible for its time, but today's cell phones make it seem useless. My stay at Cal Poly would come to an end before I could graduate. Nancy and I had been married for a few years, and a family was being planned for the near future. Work became a priority.

My wife Nancy and I started dating seriously after I came home from Spain. I had met her before I shipped off for Rota the year before. She was a talented young lady who had a great voice, played the guitar, and the piano. She went to PCC to study early childhood education, and we attended at the same time. As soon as I got my apartment, she moved in, one piece of clothing at a time. My bachelor days were numbered. We got married on July 27, 1974, in her sister's backyard on Howard Street in Pasadena, California. It was a great wedding with some of our friends playing the "Wedding Song" as she walked down the driveway. Our honeymoon was in San Diego.

For the next three years I would try to hold on to several jobs as a welder at Foremost Dairies in Los Angeles, quit out of sheer boredom, and went back to school fulltime at Cal State LA to become a teacher, until Robert our first son was born on November 15, 1977. Back to work I went again, and worked for Rockview Dairies in Downey, California, on the graveyard shift as a welder, it drove me mad. When my application to become an apprentice plumber was approved by the Burbank plumbers local, I left, and went into the construction field. The start of my plumbing career started smoothly, and I was happy to be working outdoors, but the economy started to sour. President Carter had inherited a challenging presidency, and he would not be up to the task of avoiding an economic nightmare. President Reagan took over, and my financial health took a turn for the worse. Nancy and I would hit the bottom of the financial ladder.

Justin, our second son, was born on March 12, 1981, Steven our third son came along on January 21, 1983, our family's financial health was still bleak, and to supplement my income I had remained in the US Navy Reserve after I had gotten out of active duty. I had been assigned to an attack squadron at Los Alamitos, California, but I never showed up for drills and the squadron never pursued it. When my obligated time of reserve duty ran out, a US Navy recruiter came to the house and convinced me to stay in, I would be assigned to VP-65 at Pt Mugu, California, right off Highway 1 near Ventura. I stayed with the squadron until 1977, and transferred to the Coast Guard Reserve for a change of pace. The economy hit triple digit recession, and I found myself out of work for several years. My Coast Guard pay was sporadic since it was tied in with the Department of Transportation's budget. I couldn't depend on them to send me my paychecks on time to pay my bills. So, I got out in 1980 to join the US Navy Seabees Reserve, RNMCB 16, at Chavez Ravine in Los Angeles, California, where I would stay until 1994, when I would join the California Air National Guard, 148th Combat Communications Squadron located at Ontario

Airport in California. It was a time that would bring me to the brink of utter exhaustion and mental collapse, but it would also be at one point the only finances I could get for my family. Nancy, Robert, Justin, and Steven, would always have a roof over their head, food to eat, and decent up to date clothes to wear, but it would be at a price. I would not, or could not have enough quality time to spend with them. It would haunt me well into my later years of adulthood.

The year 1983 was a turning point for me, both financially and emotionally. I had been out of work for a while, and I finally got a job working for a union outfit that was constructing the B1 bomber facilities in Lancaster, California. At last money was coming in, and we were able to pay off some of our bills. It lasted two months. Three quarters of a forty-man crew was laid off due to nepotism, the boss' son needed a job. I was one of them, but I had become friends with a fellow veteran, and he told me to contact a friend of his at the Los Angeles Unified School District who had just been promoted to plumbing supervisor and was looking for temporary plumbers. My pay would be cut by five dollars an hour, but it would be steady work. I had nothing to lose; not expecting to be hired I called and was told to go downtown to fill out an application at the personnel office; get a TB test, and come to work the next day. It was manna from heaven.

I would remain with LAUSD for twenty-six years; working my way up the promotional ladder from journeyman plumber to complex project manager until my retirement in 2009. Working at LAUSD allowed me to buy our first home in Alta Loma, California, where I still reside today. It would also be the place where I would once again be called into active duty to fight another war during Desert Shield-Desert Storm in 1991.

RNMCB 16 in 1980 was a small battalion compared to the other ones. Most of the men were Angelinos and were of Mexican heritage. They were a rough, tough bunch, but fun to drill with. For the first part of my enlistment we spent most of our drills in the reserve center at Chavez Ravine located near Dodger Stadium. Our two weeks of active duty for training were spent either in Twenty-nine Palms, Long Beach, or Port Hueneme, California. During the weekend drill we made up work to stay busy.

Shortly after I made first class petty officer things began to change. The battalion's focus became more oriented towards military training, such as small unit leadership, combat tactics, and weapons training. In 1990 I found out why. I had been working for LAUSD for seven years now and our family's finances had improved tremendously. Sometime in November, I received orders from the battalion to get my physical, and get my will and other legal paperwork in order. I was being activated for active duty with NMCB-16 for Operation Desert Shield in Southwest Asia. I was devastated.

For the next month, I was running around to the Long Beach Naval Hospital getting my physical and my medical record in order. I took time off from work to get this done. I was totally stressed out. Christmas was a month away, and I hesitated to tell Nancy and the boys that I was going on active duty. The news media had been running stories about the invasion of Kuwait by Iraq, and the US had forces standing by in the region. At work I put in the paper work for a military leave of absence. With that and my vacation time I could be expecting my full pay from LAUSD to cover our bills for a couple of months After that I would be making the salary of an E-6 in the Seabees, I was worried sick.

In December I got word that we were deploying on the 3rd of January for the Seabee base in Gulfport, Mississippi, to do our military training, and our activation ceremony to become an active Seabee battalion. Nancy had to be told. The Christmas season was a somber period for me. I tried being upbeat for her and the boys. New Years eve was the worst night ever in my life. I didn't feel much like celebrating.

On January 3, 1991, we picked up my Indo friend, who was in the battalion; we were headed for the reserve base at Los Alamitos, California. We would have to spend the night there. I still don't know the reasoning for that; we were scheduled to leave the next morning; time spent at the base could have been spent with my family. We got on the bus and headed for Ontario Airport for our flight to Gulfport. On the way there the bus got into an accident on the freeway, what a way to start a deployment. Leaving Nancy, Robert, Justin, and Steven, that day was the hardest thing I have ever done in my life; I had to hold back my tears for their sake.

We landed in Gulfport, Mississippi, on a gloomy gray day; it was freezing. What was I doing here in the first place; back in 1969 I was a young man, unmarried, no kids, and eager to go off to fight in the Vietnam War, I was naive and gung-ho. Now I was older and less enthusiastic, with a wife, three kids, and a mortgage to worry about. I was also a first class petty officer in charge of a rifle squad responsible for eleven men, and a plumbing shop to run at our next base. The responsibly of leadership weight heavily on me, and for once I took it seriously. The stakes could be tremendous.

During our first week in Gulfport we were busy working on getting our paper work in order. Then we started receiving our first set of shots, including pills to counteract chemical warfare agents. In the following days most of the men were sick with flu like symptoms; some had walking pneumonia, including myself. We spent days doing military training to get us combat ready. Most of us were out of shape physically, and the constant strain of exercising and running took its toll.

Finally the day arrived for our overseas deployment as a regular US Navy Seabee battalion. Before we boarded the plane they gave us two M-16s to carry on the plane. It seemed like overkill to me. We were told that we're going in as a standby battalion, and would be stationed at Camp Moscrip, Puerto Rico. I was elated. For the next few months I was nervous as the built up in Southwest Asia continued. There was no way they would activate a reserve battalion like ours just so we could sit around in Puerto Rico.

We landed at the airport on the military base in Puerto Rico; it was hot and dry. The breeze coming over the ocean was great. What a great country it was with palm trees, mountains, and jungles surrounding the base. The bus picked us up and took us to our battalion compound that was separate from the main base. My room was pretty decent; it looked like a motel room for one person, and was located a few yards from the ocean. It was a magnificent view. The base itself looked abandoned, it had been hit by a previous hurricane, and the start of Desert Shield didn't make things any better. It was up to NMCB-16 to get it in shape.

My future seemed to look brighter. I called Nancy that night and told her that everything was fine.

Duty in Puerto Rico was great; if there was a place to sit out the war this spot was perfect. I spent most of the time getting the base utilities, barracks, including the mess hall in tiptop shape. I had two subordinates running the plumbing and the refrigeration-air-conditioning shops. Our work schedule called for twelve-hour days for two weeks straight before we got liberty on the weekend if you didn't have a duty watch. Most of my liberty was spent in San Juan drinking, and eating the local food.

When the shooting war started, they changed the name to Desert Storm; I was at the enlisted men's club; every one cheered. I became more nervous. It was planned to be a hundred day campaign. What if it went beyond that? Nobody knew how much of a fight the Iraqi forces were going to put up. There were stories around the base that if the war lasted longer than one hundred days, we would be in trouble. The supply ships the US had were old and unreliable; once the prepositioned supplies ran out in the region, they would be hard pressed to re-supply our forces. One of the rumors had it that over ten thousand coffins were being flown in. I started smoking again, and began drinking a little more.

Life went on as usual during the war. The base was looking better, and everyone got into his or her daily work routine. I started scuba diving after having completed a certification class. Scuba diving in Puerto Rico was awesome. The waters were clear and warm. Every day after work Heinz and I would take off to a small pier in an ocean inlet located about half a mile from the compound and drink beer and fish. We had good fishing luck; it was a great way to release some stress. I also bought a bicycle to get around the base with. It was good exercise, and I lost twenty pounds riding it around.

On February 28, 1991, I heard that the war in Kuwait ended, it was right after my birthday, and I got drunk. The whole base was in a festive mood. I tried calling home, but the lines were too long. I was totally relieved. Now we would be going home, but it was not to be. We were staying put until July. I can understand now why, but then I was mad. The battalion brass wanted to have six months on active duty to get their benefits, like the GI bill, VA housing, and their overseas service ribbon. What a crock!

Some of the men had government jobs and were getting their full pay along with their military pay. They had it made. I was not, and my family was hurting financially. There were men who had their own businesses and were losing them because of their deployment. While we watched the returning troops parading as heroes in New York City, we were stuck here doing mundane jobs for someone else's so called glory.

The mundane duty in Puerto Rico followed a specific rhythm, broken only by the barbeques that the men from LA would have at the barracks. It was a great social event with delicious food, strong booze, and camaraderie. Near the end of the deployment we got a contingent of Seabees from Gulfport to train us in small unit leadership. For two weeks they had us running around in the boonies training for something we should have had before we left for war. Finally the day came for us to leave for home. Once more I had survived a war, but I wasn't looking for heroism or glory, my time for that had passed when I was young. I was thankful that we didn't have to go to Kuwait, where as a first class petty officer I would have had to send young Seabees off to get killed or maimed. Sure I would still have moments of survival guilt, but like my good friend Heinz said, "It was better to be here to sit out the war, than out in the Southwest Asian desert." How right he was.

We landed on July 4th, 1991, at Los Alamitos Reserve Center, in California, where my family and friends greeted me; it was different than before. There would still be no hero's parade, no one yelled obscenities, or spat. I walked off with my family and friends, and began my civilian life all over again.

Going back to work at LAUSD was rough. I was used to my daily routine I had in the Seabees. It would take awhile for me to adjust. The worst part was commuting to work from Alta Loma to LA. At home the boys were becoming teenagers, and they had their own weird ways of acting and doing things. Robert, Justin, and Steven, were playing in their band. It wasn't the kind of music I was used to, but it was interesting. Coming home from work, I would find a bunch of them hanging around the house in the back yard being obnoxious teenagers. They were great kids, but I was tired and upset, and got into their faces, which I regretted later on.

I stayed in the Seabees for a few more years; the money helped us get out from our financial situation. There were several two-week training tours that I went on. It probably made Nancy mad since she would have to raise the boys by herself again. She had become a stronger more independent woman while I was away during Desert Storm. I was totally impressed, and admired her for keeping our family strong. Robert, Justin, and Steven, became responsible, honorable adults because of Nancy.

Once the paychecks started coming in from LAUSD we recovered from our financial troubles. I had plans to get promoted to senior plumber, and then supervisor, which I did within five years. Being in the reserves would become a problem for me in my efforts to do this. So I decided to retire from the California Air National Guard, that I had transferred to from the Seabees in 1993, in order to enhance my career with LAUSD.

I was getting bored with the Seabees in 1993; I had reached high year tenure, which meant I could no longer get promoted because of the time I had spent in the Seabees. It was a stupid program. So I transferred to the California Air National Guard's 148th Combat Communications Squadron based near Ontario Airport, California, which was about five miles from our house. The time spent commuting less was reason enough to do this.

My job at the 148th was being a radio operator. I had completed a seven-week course for it at Keesler Air Force Base in Biloxi, Mississippi. It was an intense class. After my training, I would be deployed to several exercises with the US Army, and National Guard units as part of the total force concept that was being implemented by the military. I really enjoyed myself, and the pay too. With the guard you can get paid for doing service to the State of California and the Federal Government. I would travel more with the 148th than I did my entire career with the Seabees. This would play havoc with my work at LAUSD, not to mention Nancy, and the boys. My next deployment would alter my way of life.

My last deployment with the 148th Combat Communication Squadron was for two and a half weeks to the jungles of Bocas Del Toro province, Panama, April-May of 1996. It was an interesting tour, and I had a lot of time to visit the small villages and cities around the Panama Canal. Our base camp was located in a remote area away from Howard Air Force Base, in Panama. To get there was an hour flight on a puddle jumper. Once there, trucks would take you a few miles through the jungle to our base camp.

The camp was surrounded by thick jungle vegetation. We had US Army infantry, helicopter, Marines, and National Guard units in addition to the 148th and other combat communications squadrons. We lived in hardened tents, had access to shower and toilet facilities, a large chow hall, and a small medical facility. It was a busy camp surrounded by a river on the south side, and concertina wire around the remaining base perimeter. Outside the gate the Panamanian locals hung out.

My job was to monitor the radio traffic on the different units nets. Most of the time it was routine, except for that one day when I found an old PRC-77 radio that I had used in the Seabees. While fooling around with it, I received a call from one of the outlying post that a soldier was having an extreme asthma attack, and he didn't have his medicine. He was being rushed back in an army ambulance truck, and they wanted me to stay in contact with the driver because he couldn't contact the base medical unit.

It was my job to do this, and I contacted the medical unit on my portable telephone and explained to them what was going on. For an hour I would be relaying messages I received from the ambulance driver on the PRC-77 and relaying them to the medical unit on the phone. Apparently all went well with the soldier, and as soon as he was stabilized he would be flown out by helicopter later that evening to the main base hospital at Howard Air Force Base near the canal in Panama.

After work, I was standing around on the porch in front of our tent with some of my friends from the squadron. We were drinking beer, smoking cigarettes, and talking stories. A US Army medic came by and started talking to me. He said he recognized my voice, and asked if I had been the one on the radio when they were trying to save a soldier's life that had an asthma attack. I said yes, I was. He came up to me and told me I was a hero, and thanked me. I shook his hand, and told him I was just doing my job; it was no big deal.

Later that night as I lay under the mosquito netting in my bunk, I heard the engines of a helicopter warming up. In the darkness of the night I heard it take off and fly away over the jungle, the sound of its engines slowly disappearing in the distance. I hoped the soldier was well. After doing my job, the medic had called me a hero in front of my friends and others, but I didn't feel like one, it seemed irrelevant, for I had grown beyond my youthful dreams of heroism and glory.

After two and a half weeks in the jungles of Panama, I spent some time sight seeing around Changuinola, and the Panama

Canal. Amidst the banana plantations, the fishing villages, and along the muddy rivers, small houses stood where their impoverished occupants meeked out a living. I gave out candy at the small airport, and boarded the airplane for my flight home to Alta Loma, California. It would be my last act in the military.

I went back to work with LAUSD after my Desert Storm excursion. The mood with my supervisor was one of resentment. It wasn't any better at home. My life at home and at work was becoming unbearable. I was getting bored and frustrated at regular intervals. Something had to be done, so I took up running and lost fifty-five pounds. I decided to run the Los Angeles Marathon, and after two years of training, I completed the 1996 and 1997 marathons in less than four hours. The medals hang on the Air National Guard clock I received from the squadron, hanging on the wall near my bed, gathering dust.

After being promoted to senior plumber, I decided to retire from the military. It was a good move for me, and I would quickly move up the ladder to become a complex project manager with LAUSD. The work was exciting and fulfilling. I worked with, and observed maintenance personnel, teachers, support professionals, and school administrators at their school sites, working to improve the lives of their students in spite of insurmountable obstacles. It is because of those people that I met in my later years that my disappointment and resentment towards America and people in general has waned and started to fade. I would retire from LAUSD in 2009 a less cynical and more sensitive man.

My dad Albert passed away April 14, 2002, right after I had talked to him about taxes. My brother Edward called me a half-hour after I spoke to dad. I was numb. I miss him so much.

Bill, my father in law passed away during my stay at the Sturgis Rally in South Dakota in 2006. I took his passing the hardest. He was a Republican, a great friend, a World War II veteran, and had the same feelings of surviving war that I did. I loved him dearly.

I had come a long way from my birth in Bandung, Indonesia, as I enter my golden sunset years. It had been a long challenging trip, and I expect to have more of them. Nancy, my wife of thirty-seven years, is given all the credit by me for raising Robert, Justin, and Steven, into productive, honorable men. I am honored, and humbled by her accomplishments, and her presence.

My sisters and brothers have raised their families, and succeeded in their life's mission. They will always be my first family. I have mom and dad to thank for that.

7

Golden Sunset

My first day of retirement came on December 31, 2009; it felt weird, like a huge burden had been lifted off my shoulder. Not only would I not have to commute the dreaded freeways of Southern California, I didn't have to get up early in the morning to go to work in South Central LA. I felt a freedom that is hard to describe. Time has lost its grip on me; there would be no more scheduling and deadlines to meet. Retirement is everything I had imagined it to be.

When the LAUSD offered an early retirement, I took it without having any second thoughts. The budget crisis that the US and California was going through had affected the district also. There were to be layoffs, reduction in personnel and maintenance services, and furloughs. I saw no point in sticking around, and put in my paper work to start the process of terminating my employment with LAUSD.

Two weeks before the end of December I cleared out my office desk, my calendar, and my computer. With mixed feelings I visited my school sites and bid them farewell. It was harder for me in the office; I had worked with some of my co-workers for a long time; some were Vietnam veterans. When my last day came, I left quietly with little fanfare; the way I'm used to. As I left the maintenance area, I looked around the neighborhood, it was still rundown and ghetto looking; I would not miss it.

My retirement year of 2010 was stress free, and has given me the time needed for new adventures. I would spend my mornings sending Nancy off to work, and walk our dog Hendrix; he gives me nothing but unconditional love. Midmornings, I spend time writing, and planning for my road adventures; when noontime comes around, I go to the American Legion Post 280, in Pasadena, California.

The post cantina is where I spend most of my time when I'm not on the road, which I have done a lot this past year. I sit and drink, laugh, joke, and keep an open ear with my friends and acquaintances there. It is a dark, wooden interior canteen, unpretentious, and comfortable. I enjoy all the bartenders there, but Ray is my favorite. In the past few months, we have lost several of our brothers, may they rest in peace. As I sit there and reflect on my life, I have found that I'm no longer the disillusioned, hardened, and insentive person of my youth. I have grown into a more mellower vintage man in my golden sunset years; I'm taking the time to listen to the persons surrounding me, non opinionated, or judgmental, for they too have their own extraordinary tales to tell.

VR 24 crewmembers at the Tokyo Bar, September 1972, Roy in top row 3rd from left

Going home party in 1973. Roy at top right with beer in hand

John Adams, Roy, and Nancy in 1974

Roy and George (seated) at the 442nd Medal of Honor ceremony at Victory Park, Pasadena, California

Roy during his tour in the US Navy Seabees 1980 to 1993

Top left Dad and Roy; Top right Roy and Heinz; Bottom left Roy in San Diego; Bottom right Roy at Camp Moscrip, Puerto Rico

Roy at the 137th homecoming ceremony in Farnsworth Park, Pasadena, California

About the Author

Roy Van Westbroek was born in Bandung, on the island of Java, Dutch East Indies, in the 1950s, and grew up there until the age of seven when he and the family were relocated to Breda, Holland, and eventually ended up in Los Angeles, California, in December 1961. President John. F. Kennedy had just been elected. Raised and educated in Los Angeles, and Pasadena, Roy received his Bachelor of Arts degree in Interdisciplinary Studies from CSU Dominguez Hills in Carson, California. He served in the US Navy, and the California Air National Guard from 1969 until his retirement in 1996. Retired from public service, he now spends his time on the road with his beloved Harley.

www.ingramcontent.com/pod-product-compliance
Ingram Content Group UK Ltd.
Pitfield, Milton Keynes, MK11 3LW, UK
UKHW020126250726
13967UKWH00002B/509

9 781105 030468